FOURTH GRADE TECHNOLOGY

32 LESSONS EVERY FOURTH GRADER CAN ACCOMPLISH ON A COMPUTER

FOURTH EDITION

Part Five of the Technology Curriculum by

Structured Learning

Fourth Edition 2011
Part Five of Structured Learning's Technology Curriculum
Visit the companion website at http://askatechteacher.com for more resources to teach technology to children

To receive a free weekly digital technology tip and/or website, send an email to admin@structuredlearning.net with the message "Subscribe to Weekly Tips" or "Subscribe to Weekly Websites"

ISBN 0-9787800-4-3

Printed in the United States of America

Introduction

This Structured Learning Technology Curriculum is designed to guide you and your child through a progressive growth of age-appropriate activities, resulting in a thorough knowledge of technology appropriate to your child's age level. If you didn't start with Kindergarten, go back and start there—even if your child is in third grade. There are skills taught there that aren't covered here, because it is assumed your child already learned them.

This Fourth Grade Textbook is aligned with National Educational Technology Standards for Students (see Appendix) to insure your child receives the broadest educational training available. It is based on a time-proven method successfully used and honed in classrooms. It requires a commitment of forty-five minutes a week of uninterrupted concentration on computers, followed up with two sessions of fifteen minutes each spread out throughout the week to practice keyboarding. If you can give more—that's great! If your time doesn't allow that as so many busy families don't, your child will still accomplish every goal within this book. The only rejoinder is: If there is a skill that your child doesn't get, spend some additional time reinforcing and reminding. S/he won't get every skill the first time, but when you see it come up a second or third time through the course of these workbooks, then it's time to concentrate. Some skills are more difficult than others for some students. It doesn't mean your child can't accomplish it. It just means they need a bit of extra work.

> "The problem with computers is they do what you tell them." — *Unknown.*

The purpose of this textbook is not to teach the step-by-step details of the myriad computer skills. There are many fine books that will explain how to add Word borders, put a text box in Publisher, shade the cells in Excel and create a blog. What those books don't tell you is when your child is old enough to comprehend the skills they are teaching. That is what we do here: Guide you toward providing the right information at the right time, which allows your child the best opportunity to succeed. Just as most children can't learn to read at two, or write at four, they shouldn't be introduced to the fine motor skills of speed typing in kindergarten. We make sure your child gets what s/he needs, at the right age. The end result is a phenomenal amount of learning in a short period of time.

If there are skills that you don't know how to show your child that aren't 'taught' in this book, and you can't find books that address those in the manner you seek, you can visit the blog (AskATechTeacher.wordpress.com), the wiki and the internet start page that accompany this book (see publisher's website for more information). You'll find lots of help there.

Programs Required for K-5

Take a look at the list of programs we use. Some are free downloads (click links) or have free alternatives. The focus is programs that can collaborate with school projects, will teach critical skills, and can be used throughout the student's educational career. Here are the minimum requirements. Free alternatives are noted with links. If you don't have a pdf of this book, contact the publisher for a discounted copy:

General	(K-2)	Intermediate (3-5)
Outlook (or free Gmail)	*KidPix (or free TuxPaint)*	*MS Office (or free Open Office, Google Docs)*
Google Earth (free dl)	*Type to Learn Jr. or*	*MS Publisher*
Internet browser	*free online keyboarding*	*Adobe Photoshop (or free Gimp)*
	MS Office	*Type to Learn (or free online keyboarding)*
	MS Publisher	*Oregon Trail (free online as classic edition)*

Here's an overview of topics covered, as well as which grade. It tells you the topic, but not the skills—that comes later in this introduction. Some are covered every year, which means they are critical skills that don't go away and change with time. Some are learned early. These, once mastered, are not revisited, like mouse skills. After the addition of the second button and the scroll, not much changes with mouse skills.

	Mouse Skills	Vocabulary And Hardware	Problem-solving	Windows /Basics	Keyboard and shortcuts	Adobe Photoshop	Word	PowerPoint	Publisher	Excel	Google Earth	E-Mail	Graphics
K	☺	☺	☺	☺	☺								☺
1	☺	☺	☺	☺	☺				☺		☺		☺
2		☺	☺	☺	☺		☺	☺	☺		☺		☺
3		☺	☺	☺	☺		☺	☺	☺	☺	☺	☺	
4		☺	☺		☺		☺	☺	☺	☺	☺	☺	☺
5		☺	☺		☺	☺	☺		☺	☺	☺	☺	☺

Technology in general, and this curriculum specifically, builds on itself. What you learn a prior year will be used as you progress through the next grade level. For example, your child may have difficulty accomplishing the lessons laid out for fourth graders—say, typing 25 wpm with speed and accuracy—without going through those designated for grades K-3 sequentially. Have no fear, though: By the end of fifth grade, after following this series of lessons, they will accomplish everything necessary for Middle School.

Typical 45-minute Lesson

As you face a room full of eager faces, remember that you are a guide, not an autocrat. Use the Socratic Method—don't take over the student's mouse and click for them or type in a web address when they need to learn that skill. Even if it takes longer, guide them to the answer so they aren't afraid of how they got there. If you've been doing this since kindergarten, you know it works. In fact, by the end of kindergarten, you saw remarkable results.

When talking with students, always use the correct vocabulary. That's why I've included it on the lesson plan. Be sure to emphasize the vocabulary and expect students to understand it. Try the Vocabulary Board during one of the quarters/trimesters. Students love it and it highlights why they want to understand 'Geek Speak'.

Here's how I run a class:

- Students enter the room. They know to check the 'To Do' list on the overhead screen or Smart Board as they take their seats and plug their flash drive in. You're finishing up an email, but it doesn't matter. The beginning of class is student-directed.
- Students start with 10 minutes of typing practice, either using installed software or an online keyboarding program. Some days, they are directed to work on their site words in www.spellingcity.com or another active learning process that is self-directed.
- Next, there are three presentations (from *Google Earth Board, Problem-solving Board*, or *Vocabulary Board*). These rotate throughout the year, one per trimester/quarter. Students have selected their topic and presentation date. Whoever is up for the day will teach the class and take questions from the audience. This takes ten-twelve minutes. This week it's exploring the world with Google Earth.
- If it's the beginning of a month, I review assigned homework and take questions. If it's the end of a trimester, I review which skills have been accomplished during the last three months.
- If we are starting a new project in our year of project-based learning, I review it with them, take questions and we start. If they are in the middle of one, they use the balance of the class to work towards its completion. I monitor activities, answer questions, help where needed. They have access to installed software and the internet which makes this portion of class student-centered learning requiring critical thinking and problem-solving skills

- During their work, students are free to post vocabulary words they don't understand on the vocabulary board and problem-solving ideas on that board.
- Students who have completed the current project take advantage of 'sponge activities' from a topic of their choice, practice keyboarding for the upcoming speed quiz or help a classmate struggling with a prickly skill. I include a variety of topical websites on a class internet start page (see inset for sample). Students know any websites on this page can be used by them during sponge time.
- Students who finish early may also access the class wiki (see inset for sample) to see what they might have missed in earlier classes.

How to Achieve Your Goals on a Weekly Basis

Here's how to be sure your child gets the most out of the time s/he spends on their technology education:

- Set aside 45 minutes for the core lesson and 15 minutes twice more during the week to reinforce.
- Sit straight with body centered in front of keyboard, legs in front of body, elbows at his/her sides.
- Place both hands in home-row position even though they use only one hand at a time. Let the other rest in home position waiting for its turn.
- Set book to left of keyboard—never in front of monitor.
- Remember: Parent/teacher is the guide—not the doer!
- Don't be distracted.
- Don't blame the computer. Always take responsibility.
- Save early. Save often.
- Always make a back-up of work.
- Use tech vocabulary during lesson.
- Once a problem solution is introduced (i.e., *what's today's date*), have the student do it the next time—don't do it for them!
- Check off each lesson item as the student accomplishes it.

1. When computing, whatever happens, behave as though you meant it to happen.
2. He who laughs last probably made a back-up.
3. If at first you don't succeed, blame your computer.
4. A complex system that does not work is invariably found to have evolved from a simpler system that worked just fine.
5. A computer program will always do what you tell it to do, but rarely what you want to do.

— Murphy's Laws of Computing

TABLE OF CONTENTS

K-5 TECHNOLOGY SCOPE AND SEQUENCE

Check each skill off with I/W/M/C under '5' as student accomplishes it
(Column 1 refers to the ISTE Standard addressed by the skill)

ISTE			K	1	2	3	4	5
		I=Introduced W=Working on M=Mastered C=Connected to Classwork						
I	**Care and Use of the Computer**							
		Learn and practice safety on the Internet	I	W	W	W	M	C
		Keep your body to yourself—don't touch neighbor's kb	I	W	W	W	M	C
		Internet security—what it means, why	I	I	I	W	M	C
		Use of network file folders to save personal work	I	I	W	W	M	C
II	**Computer Hardware**							
		Understand how parts of the computer connect	I	W	M	C	C	C
		Know the names of all computer hardware	I	W	M	C	C	C
		Know how to adjust volume	I	W	M	C	C	C
		Know how to use the keyboard, mouse	I	W	M	C	C	C
		Know all parts of keyboard—Alt, F-row, space bar, etc	I	W	M	C	C	C
		Know how to turn monitor on/off	I	W	M	C	C	C
		Know how to power computer on, off	I	W	M	C	C	C
III	**Basic Computer Skills**							
		Know how to add file folders						I
		Know basic computer vocab—hardware and skills		I	W	M	C	C
		Understand Windows—desktop, icons, start button, etc.			I	W	M	C
		Understand the Ctr+Alt+Del, use of Task Manager				I	W	M
		Know how to drag-drop from one window to another						I
		Know how to log-on			I	W	M	C
		Know how to create a macro (for MLA heading)						I
		Understand mouse skills	I	W	M	C	C	C
		Understand right-click menus			I	W	M	C
		Know how to Open/Save/close a document, save-as, print	I	W	M	C	C	C
		Know how to solve common problems	I	W	M	C	C	C
		Know how to problem-solve with help files						I
		Understand tool bars in Word, Publisher, etc				I	W	M
		Know how to use flash drives—USB port, save-to, etc.				I	W	M
		Know how to use program you haven't been taught					I	W	M
		Know how to create wallpaper					I	W	M
		Understand differences/similarities between programs					I	W	M
IV	**Typing and Word Processing**							
	KB							
		Achieve age-appropriate speed and accuracy					I	W	M

		Know Alt, Ctrl, Backspace, spacebar, enter, tab, shift etc	I	W	M	C	C	C
		Know when to use cap key	I	W	M	C	C	C
		Know how to compose at keyboard		I	W	M	C	C
		Know correct spacing after words, sentences, paragraphs		I	W	M	C	C
		Use correct keyboarding posture	I	W	M	C	C	C
		Know how to use exclamation and question mark			I	W	M	C
		Understand F row				I	W	M
		Follow grammar/spelling rules	I	W	M	C	C	C
		Know when to use delete, backspace	I	W	M	C	C	C
		Know and use common keyboard shortcuts	I	W	M	C	C	C
		Know to put cursor in specific location, i.e., for graphic			I	W	M	C
		Be able to use online keyboarding sites			I	W	M	C
	WP							
		Understand Word basics			I	W	M	C
		Know how to move text within document					I	W
		Know how to use Ctrl+Enter to force a new page			I	W	M	C
		Know how to add a header/footer to a document			I	W	M	C
		Know how to format a document—fonts, borders, etc.			I	W	M	C
		Know how to use spell-check and grammar-check			I	W	M	C
		Know how to use word wrap				I	W	M
		Know how to insert pictures from clipart, file pic, internet			I	W	M	C
		Know how to insert tables				I	W	M
		Know how to insert text box						I
		Know how to create graphic organizers			I	W	M	C
		Know how to insert headers and footers			I	W	M	C
		Know how to create bullet lists and numbered lists					I	W
		Know how to outline						I
		Know print with print preview			I	W	M	C
		Know how to create and use an embedded link					I	W
		Understand Word pad, Notepad						I
V	**Designing (Photo, video, document)**							
		Introduce Digital cameras	I	I	I	I	I	I
		Know how to draw in one program and insert into another			I	W	M	C
		Insert geometric shapes into KidPix	I	W	W			
	Publisher							
		Know how to plan a publication			I	W	M	C
		Identify and understand parts of Publisher screen			I	W	M	C
		Know how to use tools, toolbars in Publisher			I	W	M	C
		Know how to add/edit text using the text box			I	W	M	C
		Know how to resize/move graphics			I	W	M	C
		Know how to use font schemes			I	W	M	C

		Know how to use color schemes			I	W	M	C
		Know how to add/delete a page, a picture or text				I	W	M
		Know how to insert a Table of Contents				I	W	M
		Know how to insert footer				I	W	M
		Know how to make a Card			I	W	M	C
		Know how to make a flier			I	W	M	C
		Know how to make a cover page				I	W	M
		Know how to make a simple storybook				I	W	M
		Know how to make a newsletter						I
		Know how to make a trifold brochure				I	W	M
		Know how to make a calendar						I
	Photoshop							
		Know how to plan a project						I
		Identify and understand the parts of the Photoshop screen						I
		Know how to use tools, toolbars in Photoshop						I
		Know how to add/edit text using the text box						I
		Know how to insert pictures (from clip art, file folder)						I
		Know how to use artistic renderings						I
		Know how to use auto fixes						I
		Know how to clone in a pic and across pictures						I
		Know how to crop with marquee, lasso tool, magic wand						I
		Know how to reset screen to default						I
		Know how to use history to go back in time						I
		Understand the use of 'layers' in constructing a project						I
		Know how to use the healing brush tool						I
		Know how to use filters						I
		Know how to replace backgrounds in pictures						I
		Know how to use 'Actions' tool on tool bar						I
		Know how to use art history brush						I
		Know how to use the paint brush						I
VI	**Presenting**							
		Introduce PowerPoint			I	W	M	C
		Understand layout, screen, tools, toolbars, placesavers			I	W	M	C
		Know how to insert text, edit, format			I	W	M	C
		Know how to insert pictures from file, internet, clip-art			I	W	M	C
		Understand how to add backgrounds to one or all slides			I	W	M	C
		Know how to insert animated GIF's/short movies			I	W	M	C
		Know how to insert animation into slides			I	W	M	C
		Know how to add transitions between slides			I	W	M	C
		Know how to add custom animations to slides			I	W	M	C
		Practice presentation skills			I	W	M	C
		Know how to have slides automatically			I	W	M	C
		Know how to insert interactive hyperlinks					I	W

	Know how to add/rearrange slides			I	W	M	C
	Know how to add music and sounds to one slide or many					I	W
	Understand and practice presentation skills			I	W	M	C
VII	**Spreadsheets**						
	Understand the layout, screen, tools, toolbars				I	W	M
	Know how to sort data				I	W	M
	Know how to format data				I	W	M
	Know how to use basic formulas				I	W	M
	Know how to recolor tabs and rename tabs				I	W	M
	Know how to widen columns and rows				I	W	M
	Know how to enter data and make a quick graph				I	W	M
	Know how to label x and y axis on graphs				I	W	M
	Know how to format a chart				I	W	M
	Know how to add a hyperlink to spreadsheet						I
	Know how to use print preview				I	W	M
	Know how to add headers/footers						I
VIII	**Internet basics**						
	Understand elements of an Internet address/URL			I	W	M	C
	Understand use of a start page	I	W	M	C	C	C
	Understand use of forward/back buttons, home, links		I	W	M	C	C
	Know how to use Bookmarks		I	W	M	C	C
	Understand difference between search and address bars	I	W	M	C	C	C
	Know how to use scroll bars	I	W	M	C	C	C
	Know how to save images and ethical considerations	I	W	M	C	C	C
	Know how to use the right click				I	W	M
	Know how to search and research on Google				I	W	M
	Know how to identify reliable sources on the internet				I	W	M
	Understand how to evaluate and identify reliable websites				I	W	M
	Web 2.0						
	Learn how to check grades online						I
	Understand Cloud computing (create a logo, avatar, etc.)				I	W	M
	Understand blogs and how to participate in them						1
	Understand an Internet start page and how to use it	I	W	M	C	C	C
	Understand internet Netiquette				I	W	M
	Understand class webpages, share info, upload files, etc.				I	W	M
IX	**Integrated — Multi-media**						
	Know how to follow directions in the use of computers	I	W	M	C	C	C
	Understand digital camera	I	W	M	C	C	C
	Know how to mix words and pictures to communicate	I	W	M	C	C	C

	Google Earth						
	Know how to find a location on Google Earth	I	W	M	C	C	C
	Know how to add a location to Google Earth's 'Places'				I	W	M
	Understand the use of latitudes and longitudes				I	W	M
	Know how to play a tour	I	W	M	C	C	C
	Know how to create a tour					I	W
	Know how to use Google Earth Community						I
	Know how to use the ruler to measure distances						I
	Email						
	Know how to email homework to teachers				I	W	M
	Understand parts of an email—subject, to, cc, message				I	W	M
	Understand and use proper email etiquette				I	W	M
	Understand the use of cc in an email				I	W	M
	Know how to attach a document to an email				I	W	M

Lesson #1—Introduction

Vocabulary	Problem solving	Collaborations
AVI *Digital* *multimedia* *Right-mouse button* *Right-click menu* *Windows* *Back-up* *PC* *USB port*	*What if double-click doesn't work (push enter* *What if monitor doesn't work (Is power on?)* *What if computer doesn't work? (move mouse around)* *Select-do (select item first, and then do what you need done)*	*"To go forward, you must backup."* *—Cardinal rule of computing*

NETS-S Standards
3. Information fluency; 4. Decision making; 5. Digital citizenship

Lesson questions? Go to http://askatechteacher.com

Review rules—tour classroom
- _____ No excuses; don't blame people; don't blame the computer
- _____ Save early, save often—about every ten minutes is a good time-frame
- _____ No food or drink around computer. Period.
- _____ Respect the work of others and yourself
- _____ Keep your hands to yourself—feel free to help your neighbor, but with words, not doing for them

Review homework policy— Homework in back of this workbook, due via email. Homework due monthly, last day of month, three due per month

Review Hardware
- _____ Mouse buttons—left and right, double click, scroll in center
- _____ CPU—power button, CD drive, USB port
- _____ Monitor—power button, screen, station number
- _____ Headphones—volume, size adjustment, connection to CPU
- _____ Keyboard—home row, F-row, enter, spacebar, Ctrl, alt, shift
- _____ Review how parts connect—behind CPU, under table, in front ports

Review 'save' and 'save-as' rules on next pages; review how to delete ('delete' key and backspace)

Take digital picture and AVI movie to be used in projects later this year. Discuss digital; discuss multimedia

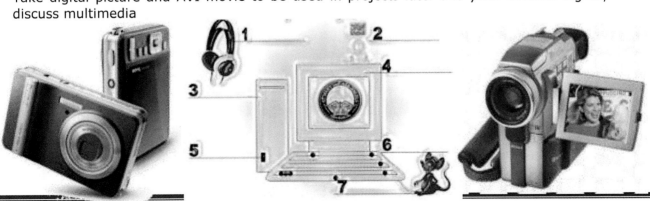

WHAT'S THE DIFFERENCE BETWEEN SAVE AND SAVE AS?

SAVE

- Save the first time
- Resave changes to the same location

SAVE AS

- Resave under a new name
- Resave to a new location

TWO WAYS

TO DELETE

BACKSPACE

Deletes to the left, one character at a time

DELETE

Deletes to the right, one character at a time

Lesson #2—Keyboarding

Vocabulary	Problem solving	Collaborations
Desktop Log-on Tool bar Protocol Wpm	My mouse doesn't work (wake it up) My volume doesn't work (check volume control on systray) Where's the right mouse? (That means the right button on mouse)	Spelling Grammar Math
NETS-S Standards: *4. Problem solving; 6. Technology concepts*		

Lesson questions? Go to http://askatechteacher.com

Review parts of computer—quiz next week (see study guide on next pages)

_____ Give students copy of the study guide on the next page. The quiz will be like this— fill it out together. Review spelling of parts—sound out, roots, prefixes and suffixes. Spelling will count because there is a word bank.

_____ Now review how parts connect to the CPU—in front and in back

_____ Advanced: Discuss what's inside computer—motherboard, etc. (see inset below)

Warm up for today's speed quiz (see sample quizzes on next few pages) with Type to Learn or online typing website. Done? Open Word for quiz

_____ Heading at top (name, date, teacher); type for five minutes

_____ While students type, walk around and observe their posture, hand position, use of fingers. Anecdotally grade them on these factors as part of speed quiz grade

_____ Spell-check (F7 or right click on red squiggly line) and correct; Find word count; type at bottom of quiz. Mental math: divide by five for wpm

_____ Review grading policy with students—grade based on improvement (see next pages for breakdown). I give Free Dress Passes (we wear uniforms) to students who meet 15wpm. This is optional. I do find students who want that prize will practice and retake the quiz in an effort to win it (I allow them to retake quizzes as often as they want without penalty).

_____ Save to network file folder; Print (Ctrl+P)

Review Homework Policy—due last day of month, at midnight, via email

_____ Homework is keyboard practice

_____ Heading/email subject line protocol: 'Lastname 4 HW#';

Dr. Seuss does technology...

If a packet hits a pocket on a socket on a port,
And the bus is interrupted as a very last resort,
And the address of the memory makes your floppy disk abort,
Then the socket packet pocket has an error to report!

If your cursor finds a menu item followed by a dash,
And the double-clicking icon puts your window in the trash,
And your data is corrupted 'cause the index doesn't hash,
Then your situation's hopeless, and your system's gonna crash!

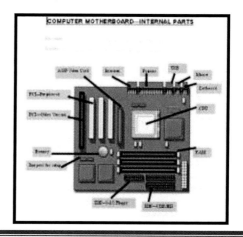

HARDWARE—PARTS OF THE COMPUTER

Name each part of the computer hardware system on the line next to it

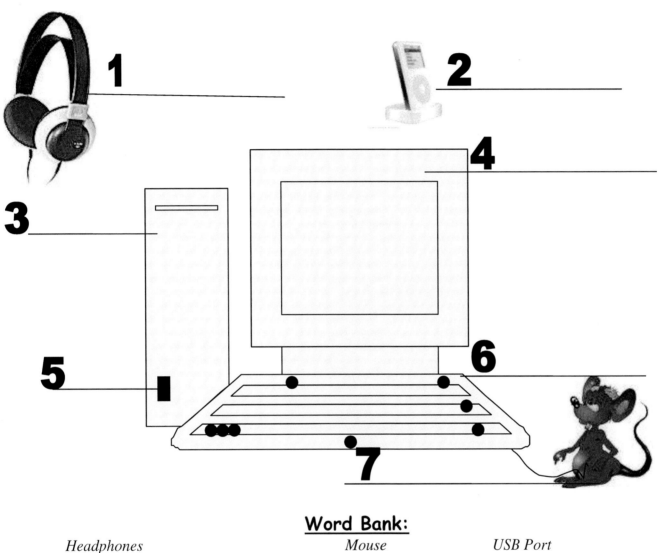

Word Bank:

Headphones	Mouse	USB Port
Keyboard	Peripheral	
Monitor	Tower/CPU	

Label the keys with a circle⬤ over them. Use this word bank:

Ctrl	Spacebar	Shift
Alt	Flying Windows	Enter
Backspace	F4	

Sample Keyboard Speed Quiz

The Best Thing In The World

Once upon a time, four princes lived in a far away land. Their father was old. One day he said, "I will not live long now. Today you must start out into the world. In a year, bring back the best thing you have found. The one who can pick the best thing shall be my new king."

The first brother said he would look in every city or town to buy the best thing for his father." The next two brothers said they would both go on fast ships over the sea to find something better.

The last brother said, "I am going to ask the people here in our own land to tell me the best thing." The other three began to laugh. "Then you will never be king!" The last brother started off. When he had gone about six miles, he met a man. "What do you carry in those big bags?" he asked. "The best thing in the world," said the man. "These are full of good nuts which fall from my five trees."

"I don't think that would work," said the brother to himself, "I must try again."

He went another seven miles and found a small brown bird. It had been hurt, so he put it in his coat where it could keep warm. As he went on, he saw a girl crying. He ran to meet her.

"Why are you crying?" he asked the little girl.

"I want to get some water from the well," she said. "We use so much. We drink cold water. We wash the clothes clean with hot water. But I do not know how to pull it up. Please show me."

The brother said, "Hold this bird and I will help you. It does not fly around anymore because it got its wing hurt."

"Thank you. What a pretty bird!" she said. "I wish you would give it to me. If you will let me keep it, I will always be very kind to it. I will take care of it myself and make it grow well."

"Yes, you may have it," said the brother.

So he gave her the bird and went on. At night, he went to sleep under a round yellow haystack. When it was light again he walked on. Every day he would walk eight or ten miles. He asked the people about the best thing in the world. Some said it was best to sing. Some said it was best to run and jump and play. Some said the green grasses were best. Some liked the red and blue and white flowers best. One man said the best thing was to ride a black horse. The Prince always stopped to help people who needed it. Soon he made many friends. All the people began to like him. They would say, "See there goes the king's son. He would be just the right kind of king for us."

Every door was open to him. The people would call to him to stop. They would ask him to come and eat with them. After he ate, he would sit down and read to the children. After he read, he showed them how to draw and write. Months went by. He still had no beautiful thing to take to his father. Just before the year was done, he went home again. The time came went he king called his sons together.

"What did you bring?" He asked them all. The other brothers had many beautiful things. "And what did you bring?" said the king to the last brother.

"This is too funny!" said the other brothers. "He has nothing!"

But the king was kind to the last brother. "What did you bring me?" the king asked again.

"I bring only the friendship of your people," said the last the brother.

"That is the best thing!" cried his father. "You shall be the new king."

This passage contains all of the 220 Dolch Basic Sight Words. Adapted from http://www.bristolvaschools.org/mwarren/DolchWords.htm

Third Grade-Fifth Grade Keyboarding Grading

By third grade, students are expected to use the good traits they've acquired in K-2 to improve keyboarding speed and accuracy. I give them a five-minute typing test once a trimester. They're graded on speed, accuracy, and good typing habits. As they type, I walk around and anecdotally judge their posture, hand position, use of fingers, etc and deduct points if they are inadequate.

At the end of the five-minute quiz, I allow one minute to correct spelling errors using a right-click on the red squiggly lines.

Grading is based on improvement from their last quiz. A student who types 10 wpm could get a 7/10 if he didn't improve or a 10/10 if he improved from 8wom on the last quiz. Here's the breakdown:

20% improvement:	*10/10*
10% improvement:	*9/10*
1-10% improvement:	*8/10*
No improvement:	*7/10*
Slowed down:	*6/10*

I post a list of keyboard speedsters in each class on the bulletin board. I also post the winning class (fastest) for all to see. Students who reach the grade level standard for speed and accuracy get a free dress pass (we are a uniform school). This is quite exciting for them:

Grade level standards are:

K-2	*None*
3rd Grade:	*15 wpm*
4th Grade:	*25 wpm*
5th Grade:	*30 wpm*

KEYS YOU SHOULD KNOW

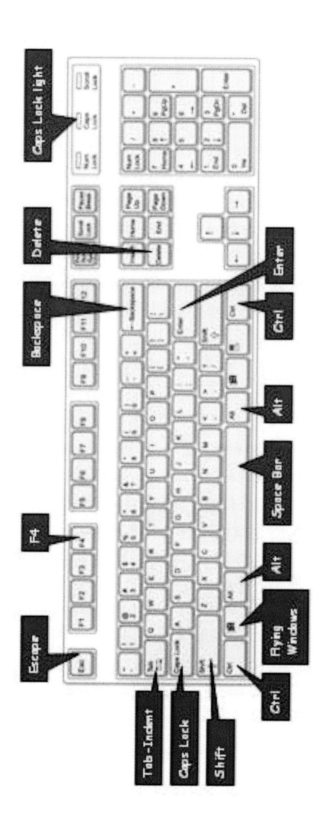

Assume the Position

- Legs centered in front of body
- Body centered in front of keyboard
- Elbows at sides
- Hands curved over home row
- Document to left of computer
- Use right thumb for space bar
- Eyes on screen

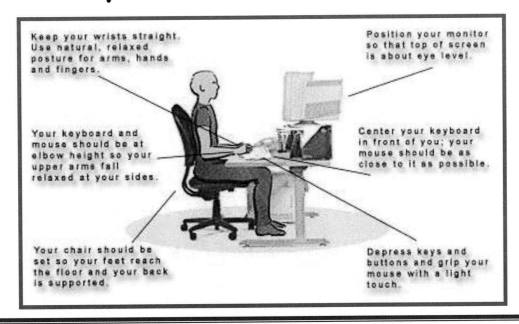

These keyboarding hints came directly from the classroom, tested on 400 students a year. These are the most common fixes that help students excel at keyboarding"

1. Tuck elbows against sides of your body. This keeps hands in the right spot—home row
2. Use your thumb for the space bar. That leaves hands on home row
3. Curl fingers over home row—they're cat paws, not dog paws
4. Use inside fingers for inside keys, outside fingers for outside keys
5. Use the finger closest to the key you need. Sounds simple, but this isn't what usually happens with beginners.
6. Keep pointers anchored to f and j
7. Play keyboard like a piano (or violin, or guitar, or recorder). You'd never use your pointer for all keys
8. Fingers move, not your hands. Hands stay anchored to the f and j keys
9. Don't use caps lock for capitals! Use shift.
10. Add a barrier between sides of the keyboards. I fashioned one from cover stock. That'll remind students to stay on the correct side of keyboard

Lesson #3—Intro to Google Earth

Vocabulary	Problem solving	Collaborations
• *Power button* • *Alt* • *F4* • *Etiquette* • *Email* • *Cc* • *Urgent*	• *My monitor doesn't work (Check power button)* • *How do I close a program (Alt+F4)* • *How do I move between cells (tab)* • *Where's 'bcc'? (click 'cc' and it shows up)*	• *Grammar* • *Spelling* • *Geography*

<u>NETS-Standards</u>
2. Communication and collaboration; 3. Information fluency; 6. Technology concepts:

Lesson questions? Go to http://askatechteacher.com

Hardware Quiz— Any questions before beginning (see sample under Lesson 2)

_____ Give ample time, but not too much to get frustrated

_____ If a student didn't do as well as they hoped, allow them to retake for full credit. Few will and those that do will work extra-hard to do better the next time.

Outlook (or Gmail)—review with sample email (reminder of 3rd grade skills)

_____ *To* and *cc*—very important to spell address correctly

_____ Review *Subject*, body of email, attachment, urgent flag

_____ Email etiquette—go over rules (see next page)

_____ Ask students to review the hand-out with their parents

Lesson Plan—Google Earth can be used for many classroom activities. It is a favorite of even my kindergartners. In this lesson, start by reviewing 2nd/3rd grade skills—how to pan in and out, drag to move the globe, change the perspective of the earth's surface, locate major latitudes and longitudes, how to find countries along the same latitude/longitude. Then, have students find animals on different continents to support classroom discussion on animals.

_____ Open program. Have students activate Google Earth lats and longs with 'view', 'grid'. Have students play Google Earth tour created by last year's fifth graders to browse this wonderful mapping program.

_____ Have students take Google Earth tours you've installed of animals around the world (see suggested sites in appendix or check Google Earth community). Encourage them to pause tour to explore an interesting animal or environ. Give ample time to associate an animal with its habitat. Discuss why cold environs evolve animals with lots of fur. What types of animals thrive in forests?

_____ Alternatively, provide students with a digital list of animals and their continents—have students find them around the globe.

_____ Fill out worksheet (see next pages) with two countries on each lat/long and the animals that live there. Do the first with students.

_____ Allow them to collaborate with neighbors. Walk around to help them when they have trouble finding country names or the home continents of animals.

_____ Turn sheet in at end of class.

Bring science book next week to outline

EMAIL ETIQUETTE

1. Use proper formatting, spelling, grammar
2. CC anyone you mention
3. Subject line is a quick summary of what email discusses
4. Use correct subject line protocol—lastname-grade-topic (lastname3hw2)
5. Answer received emails swiftly
6. Re-read your email before sending
7. Don't use capitals—THIS IS SHOUTING
8. Don't leave out the subject line
9. Don't attach unnecessary files
10. Don't overuse high priority
11. Don't email confidential information
12. Don't email offensive remarks
13. Don't forward chain letters or spam
14. Don't open attachments from strangers

Latitude Practice

Open Google Earth. Find two continents that cross each of the major Latitudes and Longitudes. Write them on the line next to that latitude and longitude.

Take Google Earth tours of Habitats and World Animals or find animals on the list provided. As you're working, write down two animals that live on each continent. Click on the animal for more information and to watch videos of the animal.

1. Equator _____
   a. Animal #1:_____
   b. Animal #2:_____
2. Tropic of Cancer_____
   a. Animal #1:_____
   b. Animal #2:_____
3. Arctic Circle_____
   a. Animal #1:_____
   b. Animal #2:_____
4. Tropic of Capricorn_____
   a. Animal #2:_____
   b. Animal #1:_____
5. Antarctic Circle_____
   a. Animal #1:_____
   b. Animal #2:_____
6. Prime Meridian_____
   a. Animal #1:_____
   b. Animal #2:_____

Lesson #4—Outlining in MS Word I

Vocabulary	Problem solving	Collaborations
Outline *Bullets* *Alignment* *Caps lock* *Monitor* *Double click* *Icons*	*Computer doesn't work (wiggle the mouse; check monitor power)* *Capital doesn't work (Is your caps lock on?)* *What is today's date (check clock in lower right corner)* *How do I exit a program (Alt+F4)*	*Science* *Language A* *Geography* *Outlining*

<u>NETS-S Standards:</u>
3. Information fluency; 4. Critical thinking; 6. Technology operations

Lesson questions? Go to http://askatechteacher.com

Keyboarding—Type to Learn or online typing program

_____ Correct posture, hand position, legs in front of body

Sign up for Problem Solving Board—start next week (see next pages)

_____ Sign up for a problem to solve. Students can get the solution from family, friends, neighbors or even the teacher as a last resort. They are responsible for teaching their classmates how to solve the problem.

_____ Sign up for a date to present. They will tell their classmates their problem, how to solve it and take questions. It takes only about three minutes.

_____ Review how you'll grade them (see next pages)

_____ Students can sign up before/after school, lunch, any time they're free.

Review problems students should know how to solve as intro to Board (see next pages).

Include shortkeys—students love these. They're easier than finding tools

Lesson Plan— Teach students how to outline using MS Word's ridiculously simple outline tools (bullet list, tab and shift+tab). Use any textbook or notes. Help them to get started, and then let them figure it out themselves.

_____ Put heading at top (name, teacher, date); Center title beneath heading

_____ Use three ribbon tools: bullet or numbered list, increase indent to push text to the right (subpoint), decrease indent to push text to left (more important point)

_____ Or, use tab to indent and Shift+tab to outdent—I like this better

_____ Outline chapter headings, subheadings

_____ Close down to desktop using 'x' or Alt+F4

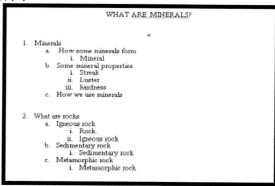

Problem Solving Board Sign-up

	Teacher #1	Teacher #2	Teacher #3
Week of October 2nd			
Week of October 9th			
Week of October 16th			
Week of October 23rd			
Week of October 30th			
Week of November 6th			
Week of November 13th			
Week of November 27th			

	Teacher #1	Teacher #2	Teacher #3
What if the double-click doesn't work			
What if the monitor doesn't work			
What if the volume doesn't work			
What if the computer doesn't work			
What if the mouse doesn't work			
What's the right-mouse button for?			
What keyboard shortcut closes program			
How do I move between cells/boxes?			
How do I figure out today's date?			
What if the capital doesn't work			
What if my toolbar disappears			
What if the document disappears			
Keyboard shortcut for 'undo'			
How do I search for a file			
What if the program disappears			
What if the program freezes			
What is the protocol for saving a file			
What is protocol for email subject line			
What does 'CC' mean in an email			
How do I exit a screen I'm stuck in			
How do I double space in Word			
How do I add a footer in Word			
How do I add a watermark in Word			
How do I make a macro in Word			
How do I add a border in Word			
How do I add a hyperlink in Word			
Keyboard shortcuts for B, I, U			

PROBLEM SOLVING BOARD
GRADING

Name: _____

Class: _____

Knew question   _____

Knew answer   _____

Asked audience for help if didn't know answer _____

No umm's, stutters   _____

No nervous movements (giggles, wiggles, etc.) _____

Overall   _____

Common problems students face using computers

	Problem	Solution
1	My browser is too small	Double click the blue bar
2.	Browser tool bar missing	Push F11
3.	Exit a program	Alt+F4
4.	Today's date	Hover over clock Shift+Alt+D in Word
5.	Double click doesn't work	Push enter
7.	Start button disappeared	Use Windows button
8.	Program disappeared	Check taskbar
9.	Erased my document	Ctrl+Z
10.	I can't find a tool	Right click on screen; it'll show most common tools
11.	My screen is frozen	Clear a dialogue box Press Escape four times
12.	My menu command is grey	Press escape 4 times and try again
13.	Can't find Bold, Italic, Underline	Use Ctrl+B, Ctrl+I, Ctrl+U

UNDO

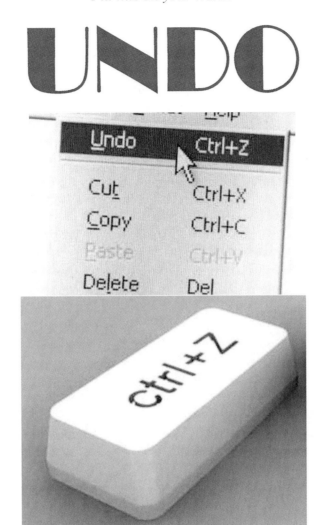

is your Friend

Popular shortkeys students love using:

Maximize window   Double click title bar

Quick Exit   Alt+F4

Date and Time   Shift+Alt+D = Date
    Shift+Alt+T = Time

Show taskbar   WK (Windows key)

Shows desktop   WK+M

Ctrl Key Combinations

CTRL+C: Copy   CTRL+K: Add hyperlink

CTRL+X: Cut   CTRL+E: Center align

CTRL+V: Paste   CTRL+L: Left align

CTRL+Z: Undo   CTRL+R: Right align

CTRL+B: Bold   CTRL+ : Zoom in Internet

CTRL+U: Underline   CTRL- : Zoom out

CTRL+I: Italic   Internet

CTRL+P: Print

Fun Keyboard Shortcuts:

< + = + > = ⇔

— + > = →

:+) = ☺

Add Your Favorite:

_____

_____

Sample Chapter Outline

Student name

Teacher

Date

<u>Climates And How They Change</u>

1. Climate
    a. Temperature
        i. Add a note
        ii. Add another note
    b. Humidity
    c. Atmospheric pressure
    d. Wind rain
2. World Climates
    a. Polar zone
        i. Name an animal
    b. Mountain zone
    c. Temperate zone
    d. Tropical zone
    e. Desert zone
        i. Name an animal
3. Climate changes
    a. El Nino
    b. Ice age
4. Human affect on climate
    a. Greenhouse effect
    b. Global warming
    c. Seeding clouds

Lesson #5—Outlining in Word II

Vocabulary	Problem solving	Collaborations
Font	*My numbers disappeared on my outline (backspace until you're back into outline; push enter—it'll add next number*	*Grammar*
Alignment		*Spelling*
Ribbon		*Science*
Tools		*Critical thinking*
Menu bar	*I can't close down (Alt+F4)*	*Problem-solving*
Task bar	*My document disappeared (try Ctrl+Z)*	
Drop-down menus	*I can't find my file (go to Start-search)*	
Formatting		

NETS-S Standards:
1. Creativity and innovation; 4. Critical thinking; 6. Technology operations

Lesson questions? Go to http://askatechteacher.com

Keyboarding— Type to Learn or online typing program

_____ Correct posture, hand position, legs in front of body

Remember: Homework due the end of each month

Start Problem solving board. Be encouraging to students—this is difficult. Even when they know the answer, it's difficult to be the 'teacher'

Continue Word project on Outlining; students can work independently from wherever they left off last week

_____ Review outlining using Word—use three tools on ribbon

_____ Use numbering tool, decrease indent and increase indent, or tab to indent, shift+tab to exdent

_____ Done? Check for spelling, grammar, correct indents

_____ Save to network file; save-as to flash drive. What's the difference between 'save' and 'save-as'?

_____ Print (Ctrl+P); close with Alt+F4.

Those who finished, go to 'sponge sites' (see list on next pages)

_____ List these on the class internet start page (click link to see mine or go to http://www.protopage.com/smaatech#Untitled/Fourth Grade) or the class webpage. All should be sites that can be enjoyed in 5-10 minute segments

_____ Students can go to a category being covered in class or a general category-of-interest (i.e., art, geography)

_____ See appendix for suggestions of sites

"A computer does what you tell it to do, not what you want it to do."

WHAT ARE MINERALS

1. Minerals
   a. How some minerals form
      i. Mineral
   b. Some mineral properties
      i. Streak
      ii. Luster
      iii. Hardness
   c. How we use minerals

2. Types of rocks
   a. Igneous rocks
      i. Rocks
      ii. Igneous rocks

Lesson #6—Internet Research

Vocabulary	Problem solving	Collaborations
Right-click *Desktop* *Background* *Image* *Search* *Hits* *Graphic organizer*	*What if password doesn't work? (Did you spell it correctly?)* *How do I open a program (Start-all programs)* *How do I close a program (Alt+F4)*	*Science* *Critical thinking* *Analyzing and organizing information*
NETS-S Standards: *3. Research and information fluency; 6. Technology concepts*		

Lesson questions? Go to http://askatechteacher.com

Type to Learn or online typing website. Watch posture, hand position; eyes on screen
Continue with Problem Solving Board

Lesson plan—Show students how to use Google search tools to research, find specific files. Use Google to convert money, find the time around the world, add, define a word and more. Students have a lot of fun trying the different skills.

_____ Open Google.com; discuss difference between search bar and address bar
_____ Discuss the make-up of a website address (see next pages)
_____ Type *California Missions* or a topic students are studying in their classroom (no quotes) into the search bar. Notice how many hits it gets.
_____ Now type "California missions" (with quotes)—quotes refine hits
_____ Now type "California missions" indians—adding a word refines hits more
_____ Now type "California missions" –'santa barbara'—the 'minus' sign leaves out sites about that word
_____ Look at the hits—notice the extensions—.org, .gov, .edu, .net, .com. Discuss how knowing the extension helps select the most reliable sites
_____ Try other search skills listed on next page—find definitions, find names in the phonebook, use calculator functions, convert currencies, find area codes and specific file types, find specific site types and similar sites, find the time around the world and use * as a general term. Students have fun with this.
_____ Explore for locations of different biomes, from USA and worldwide
_____ Save all sites to 'favorites' for easy access next week

Close to desktop

HOW TO SEARCH ON GOOGLE

Definitions	Define: computer definitions of the word computer from Web.
Phonebook	Phonebook: Murray Irvine Phonebook for people named 'murray' in Irvine
Calculator	33+33 provides the answer to any function
Converter	Converts currencies. I.e., 45 US dollars in yen
Area Code Finder	'949' shows geographic location with this area code
File type finder	'civil war filetype:ppt finds PowerPoints on Civil War
Site type finder	'Site edu lincoln' finds .edu websites about Lincoln 'site:UK Iraq' finds British websites about Iraq
Similar sites	type "related:" followed by the website address: 'related:www.google.com'
License plate finder	Type plate number into search bar
Time finder	'time in New York' tells you current time in New York
Fill in the blank	Use asterisk in sentence and Google will fill it in with the correct information. I.e., Mt. Everest is * feet high.

Error, no keyboard. Press F1 to continue.

ELEMENTS OF WEB ADDRESS

You enter the site's URL by typing it into the **Location** bar of your web browser, just under the toolbar.

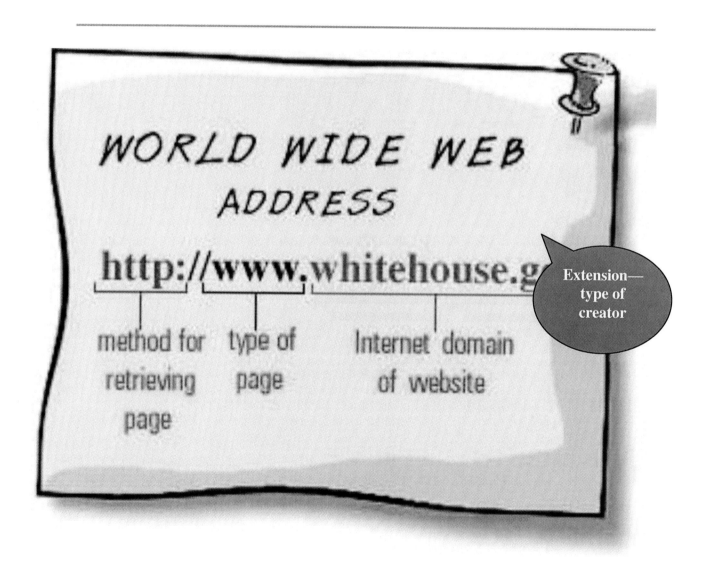

If you type...	You will find pages containing...
Hawaii Vacation	Webpages with the words **Hawaii** and **vacation**
Maui OR Hawaii	Webpages with the word **Maui** or **Hawaii**
"To each his own"	Webpages with the exact phrase **"to each his own"**
Virus –computer	Webpages with the word **virus** but NOT **computer**
"Star Trek" fan	Webpages with the phrase **"Star Trek"** and fan
To find info, type it as a sentence with an asterisk for the unknown.	

HOW TO SEARCH ON GOOGLE

Definitions	Define:word; internet definitions of a word, i.e., define:computer
Phonebook	Phonebook:Harris Irvine; a white pages list of people named "Harris' in Irvine
Calculator	33 + 33 provides answer to any function (+, -, *, /)
Converter	Converts currencies. I.e., '45 US dollars in yen'
Area Code Finder	'949' shows geographic location with this area code
File type finder	filetype:ppt "Civil War" finds PowerPoints on Civil War
Site type finder	Site:edu lincoln finds .edu websites about Lincoln
Similar sites	related:website.com finds websites similar to the one entered; i.e.,; 'related:www.google.com'
License plate finder	Type plate number into search bar
Time finder	'time in New York' tells you current time in New York
Fill in the blank	Use asterisk in sentence and Google will fill it with the correct information. I.e., 'Mt. Everest is * feet high.

Thirty-two Ways to Use Spare Classroom Time

I keep a list of themed websites that are easy-in easy-out for students. They must be activities that can be accomplished enjoyably in less than ten minutes. In the parlance, these are called "sponges".

You may have read my post with <u>nineteen sites my students love visiting</u> during sponge time (let me know if you liked them, have some to add, I'm always interested in learning from you). Here are thirty-two more. Hope you like them!

Language Arts

- <u>Make your own Story</u>—answer questions, and the story writes itself
- <u>Funny poetry</u> to read and enjoy
- <u>Jeff's Poetry for Kids</u>
- <u>Fill in the blank poetry</u>
- <u>Get Writing</u>—write your own story
- <u>Web version of Mad Libs</u>

Math

- <u>Math and Virtual Manipulatives</u>
- <u>Math website</u>—popular, a standard
- <u>Math—by Grade Level</u>
- <u>Math—game-oriented</u>
- <u>Mental Math</u>
- <u>Minute Math</u>

Research

- <u>All-around research site</u>
- <u>Research for kids</u>
- <u>School Tube</u>—learning videos organized by topics
- <u>World Book Online</u>

- <u>Research</u>—chapters on subjects
- <u>National Geographic for kids</u>
- <u>Nova video programs</u>

Science

- <u>Videos on science topics</u>
- <u>Visit a Virtual Farm</u>
- <u>Virtual weather, machines and surgery</u>
- <u>National Geographic Kids</u>
- <u>NOVA Videos</u>—great topics Nova video programs
- <u>Science Headlines</u>—audio (grades 3+)
- <u>Great site on yucky stuff</u>
- <u>Virtual tours</u>

Technology

- <u>Virtual tours</u>
- <u>Webcams around the World</u>
- <u>More Worldwide webcams for kids</u>
- <u>Nova video programs</u>
- <u>School Tube</u>—learning videos from YouTube. Organized by topics

Lesson #7—Graphic Organizers

Vocabulary	Problem solving	Collaborations
▪ Diagram ▪ Taskbar ▪ Toggle ▪ Fill ▪ Organizer	▪ What if program disappears (look on taskbar)? ▪ What is today's date?(Shift+Alt+D) ▪ I can't find my document/my file folder (Start button-search)	▪ Grammar ▪ Spelling ▪ Science
NETS-S Standards: 2. Communication; 3. Research and information fluency		

Lesson questions? Go to http://askatechteacher.com

Type to Learn or online typing website—goal is 25 wpm by the end of 4th grade

_____ Correct posture, legs in front; hands curved over home row; elbows at sides

Continue with Problem Solving Board

Remember: Homework due end of each month (see Appendix for Homeworks)

Lesson Plan—Use Word's SmartArt diagrams to display an idea in a picture format. Between grades 2-5, I use the pyramid, the arrows, spokes and wheel, and the target. Once the data is filled in, show students how to format

_____ Open Word with blue W on desktop

_____ Insert-SmartArt; Select a wheel-and-spokes graphic organizer (see sample below)

_____ Add shapes until you have 5 to 8, depending upon your project; put your biome (i.e., 'Desert') or 'Biome' in center shape

_____ Open internet (notice Word is still open on taskbar—that's good)

_____ Add 5 famous examples of your biome (or five fast facts), or add all worldwide biomes to shapes around center

_____ On SmartArt ribbon, change colors and style as you like

_____ Advanced: change the fill to a biome picture (see samples below). This is easy.

Advanced: Share the same3 information in a table (see sample on next pages)

_____ Save (Ctrl+S); save-as to flash drive. What's the difference? Print (Ctrl+P). Remind students of the table they did in third grade.

Close down to desktop (Ctrl+S to save, and Alt+F4 to close)

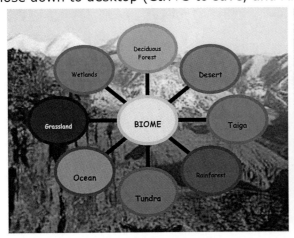
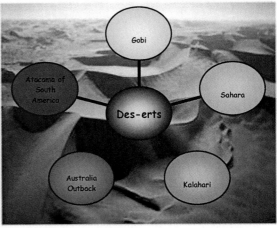

BIOME TABLE

Biomes	Example	Picture
Fresh Water	Lake Michigan Nile River Ponds	
Oceans	Pacific Ocean Indian Ocean	
Deciduous forest	Redwood Forest Canadian Forest	
Desert	Gobi Desert Sahara Desert	
Grassland	African Savanna Colorado prairie	
Rainforest	Amazon Southeast Asia	

Lesson #8—Halloween Greetings

Vocabulary	Problem solving	Collaborations
Clip-art Font Cursor Blinking Tool bar Log-on Red 'X' Format Watermark	What if double-click doesn't work? (push enter) What if program disappears (look on taskbar)? Save early, save often It's hard to highlight a word (click inside the word and then format)	Spelling Grammar Composition
NETS-S Standards: 1. Creativity and innovation; 6. Technology operations		

Lesson questions? Go to http://askatechteacher.com

Problem-solving Board—continue with presentations

Lesson plan: Students write a brief story in MS Word using writing traits studied in the classroom. Use this project to review MS Word skills. Add multiple fonts, font sizes, font colors, a border, pictures, and a watermark if possible.

_____ Open MS Word without assistance. Put heading at top of page (name, date, teacher). Type a short story in Times New Roman 18 font.

_____ Add title using WordArt, then add a festive border—both with minimal assistance.

_____ Change font, font color and font size for 5 words (click inside word, use appropriate tool on ribbon)—again, with minimal assistance.

_____ Insert 5 pictures to go along with your story; resize as needed

_____ Insert watermark that says 'Happy Halloween'. This is a new skill, so demonstrate first and then have students do it themselves. Instead of text, they may choose to add a holiday picture.

_____ Insert a footer with student name. Explain the purpose of a footer. This story doesn't need one, but you want students to learn the skill

_____ Spell check; print preview—does story fit on one page? Resize images as needed. Complete check list to be sure all skills are included (see next pages)

_____ Save to your file folder; save-as to flash drive. Why 'save' once and 'save-as' the second time?

_____ Print (Ctrl+P)

Done? Students go to class start page; select a website that correlates with classroom inquiry or classroom math instruction. See appendix for suggestions.

HALLOWEEN STORY

Your name_____

Your teacher_____

Date_____

The Orange Bat

Once there was a **Big** orange **bat** who

lived in a **HAUNTED HOUSE**. He scared

everyone away who wanted to move in, but one

man would not leave. He found the **Big**

orange **bat** and said to him, "We will

scare people together on

Halloween." And that's what they

did.

The End

HALLOWEEN STORY—GRADING RUBRIC

Name_____

Date_____

Teacher's Name_____

1. Heading with name, date, teacher   _____
2. Several lines of story   _____
   a.   5 different fonts   _____
   b.   5 different size fonts   _____
   c.   5 different colors   _____
   d.   Spell-check   _____
   e.   Grammar check   _____
3. A festive border   _____
4. A WordArt title   _____
5. 5 pictures—all the same size   _____
6. Footer   _____
7. Story fills page, but not more   _____
8. Check Print Preview   _____
9. Professional appearance   _____

Q: What was the witch's favorite subject in school?

A: Spelling
http://www.kidsdomain.com/holiday/halloween/games/jokes.html

An alternative to the holiday story is this MS Word Assessment. Use the graph on the next page to evaluate their skills. Then you'll know what they remember and what they need work on:

Your name
Your teacher
Today's Date

WORD ASSESSMENT

Follow the instructions below. Part of the assessment is how well you read and complete directions. Do your best. If you don't remember how to do a skill, go on to the next.

- Put your heading on page
- Right-align heading
- Put a title underneath heading——"Word Assessment"
- Center the title, font Comic Sans, font size 14, bold
  - Type two paragraphs about your summer, font size 12, Times New Roman
- Change the second paragraph to font size 16 and Papyrus
- Add bullets with
  1. Your daily activities
  2. What you ate
  3. Who you played with
- Add "The End" as WordArt at the bottom of the page
- Add a border

This is easy!!!

> *Wherever you are, be there until you leave.*
> *—mom*

- Add a picture
- Have text wrap around the clipart
- Put a call-out aimed at the picture
- Add an autoshape
- Color the autoshape pink or red
- Insert a footer
- Add a text box with what your mom said the most this summer
- Shade the text box
- Add a table with seven columns and three times during the day
- Add information for each day and each time of day

Sunday	Monday	Tuesday	Wednesday	Thursday	Friday	Saturday
Ate breakfast						
Ate lunch						
Ate dinner						

WORD ASSESSMENT

Question		1	2	3	4	5	6	7	8	9	10	11	12	13	14	15	16	17	18	19	20
										STUDENT											
1	heading																				
	all parts																				
2	right align																				
3	title																				
	underneath																				
4	center																				
	Comic sans																				
	size 14																				
	Bold																				
5	2 paragraphs																				
	size 12																				
	TNR																				
6	Para. 2																				
	size 16																				
	Papyrus																				
7	bullets																				
	daily activities																				
	ate																				
	played w/																				
8	The End																				
	Wordart																				
	page bottom																				
9	border																				
10	picture																				
11	text wrap																				
12	call-out																				
	location																				
13	autoshape																				
14	pink																				
15	footer																				
16	text box																				
	mom's words																				
17	shade text box																				
18	table																				
	7 columns																				
	3 rows																				
	heading row																				
19	table into																				
Total		0	0	0	0	0	0	0	0	0	0	0	0	0	0	0	0	0	0	0	0

Using an Internet Start Page

An internet start page is the first page that comes up when students select the
internet icon. It should include everything students visit on a daily basis
(typing websites, research locations, sponge sites) as well as information
specific to the current project, class  guidelines, the day's 'to do' list, and a calculator. It is one of the great ways
teachers can make internetting simpler and safer for their students.

Mine includes oft-used websites, blog sites, a To Do list, search tools, email, a
calendar of events, pictures of interest, rss feeds of interest, weather, news, a
graffiti wall and more. Yours will be different. I used protopage.com, but you can
use netvibes or pageflakes.com. Each comes with its own collection of installable
'widgets' to personalize the page to your needs.

Start pages are an outreach of the ever-more-
popular social networking. Most search engines
offer them also (try iGoogle at
www.google.com/ig). They all have a huge library
of custom fields (called 'flakes' on Pageflakes) to
individualize any home page. And, they're all simple. Don't be intimidated.

When you get yours set up, on the To Do list, put what the child should do to start
each computer time. This gives them a sense of independence, adultness, as they
get started while you're wrapping something else up.

Lesson #9—MS Word Tables I

Vocabulary	Problem solving	Collaborations
Columns Rows Cells Tab 4x5 Handles	I deleted my work (Ctrl+Z) What's today's date (Shift+Alt+D) I ran out of rows! (click in last cell of table and push tab) There's not enough room—keep typing; cell increases in size	Grammar Spelling Social studies Geography Science

NETS-S Standards:
2. Communication; 3. Research; 4. Critical thinking

Lesson questions? Go to http://askatechteacher.com

Keyboard—Type to Learn or online typing program; Good posture and hand position
Problem-solving Board presentations continue

Lesson Plan—In this geography lesson, students use Word to design a four-column table on ecosystems (or another topic being discussed in the classroom). Collect data as a group while the class discusses ecosystems. Great lesson to coordinate with the classroom unit of inquiry as students learn how to make tables in Word and import pictures.

_____ Place heading at top of page—name, teacher, date; use keyboard shortcut for date (Shift+Alt+D)
_____ Center title 'Ecosystems'; use #16 font, caps lock, bold
_____ Add 4x5 table—we'll add extra rows if we need
_____ Basics: Remember table skills from 3rd grade. Tab moves right, shift+tab moves left, enter to move to a second line in the cell; tab in the last cell of table adds a new row
_____ Add column headings—'Ecosystems', 'Example', 'Definition', 'Picture'. 14 font, bolded, centered; shade row so it stands out
_____ Discuss: What are ecosystems? How are they different from landforms?
_____ Fill in first three columns of table during the discussion
_____ Check grammar and spelling using red and green squiggly lines.
Save to file folder; save-as to flash—what's the difference between 'save' and 'save as'?

ECOSYSTEMS

Ecosystems	Example	Definition	Picture
Mountain	Himalayas, Mount Everest, Mount St. Helens, Yosemite, Yosemite, Ridgecrest, South Lake Tahoe	Earth's Higher Landforms	
Coast	L.A. San Francisco, Laguna Beach, San Francisco, Oakland	Where Land and Water Meet	
Central Valley	San Joaquin Valley, Imperial Valley, Sacramento, Fresno, Stockton, Modesto	The Center of California Where Many of the country occurs agriculture	
Desert	Palm springs, Langscape El Centro India	A Big arid and featureless climate has a lot of life	

> "A printer consists of three main parts: the case, the jammed paper tray and the blinking red light"

Lesson #10—MS Word Tables II

Vocabulary	Problem solving	Collaborations
• Clipboard • Tool • Crop • Toggle • Format picture • Wrap • Concurrent	• My capitals are stuck on (Is it your caps lock?) • How do I log on (user name, password) • Save early-save often(every ten minutes) • Internet picture is hard to work with (did you grab thumbnail?)	• Grammar • Spelling • Science
NETS-S Standards: 1. Creativity and innovation; 3. Research and information fluency		

Lesson questions? Go to http://askatechteacher.com

Type to Learn or online typing website (see appendix for suggestions)

_____ Use good posture, correct hand placement, elbows at sides

Problem solving Board—finish presentations

Open Word tables started last week

_____ Finish entering ecosystems data into first 3 columns

_____ Go to Google; search for image of first ecosystem

_____ Select one that communicates the environ and copy to clipboard. Explain 'clipboard' to students—that anything on it can be pasted into a variety of programs. Show students how to bring it up from the MS Office ribbon (from the 'home' menu). If there's time, show how it pastes into, say, PowerPoint

_____ Toggle back to Word table on taskbar; right-click-paste image into cell; resize as needed to fit the cell. Repeat for each ecosystem picture

_____ Use crop tool (cross-hatch tool) to remove any part of picture you don't need

_____ Trouble moving the image? Select 'Picture Tool' from top of screen; select 'Wrap'; select 'in front of'

_____ Done? Check print preview to be sure everything fits on one page.

_____ Save (Ctrl+S), print (Ctrl+P)

Close down to desk top with Alt+F4

Those who finish, go to class internet start page. Have a list of websites for them to visit that correlate with the discussion on ecosystems. See appendix for ideas.

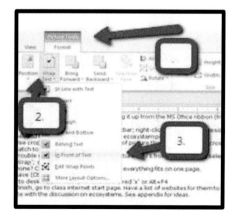
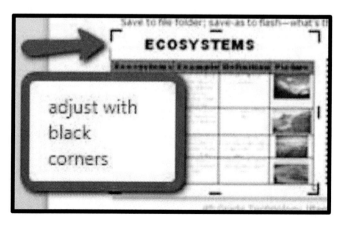

Lesson #11—Thanksgiving Greetings

Vocabulary	Problem solving	Collaborations
Template *Text box* *Ctrl+S* *Ctrl+P* *Schemes*	*I can't find a tool bar (right-click in the toolbar area)* *I can't find a tool (click the double arrow at the end of the toolbar)*	*Spelling* *Grammar* *Science—ecosystems* *Art—graphics*
NETS-S Standards: *1. Creativity and innovation; 3. Research; 4. Critical thinking*		

Lesson questions? Go to http://askatechteacher.com

Type to Learn or online typing website. Remember goal: 25 wpm by the end of the year

_____ Check posture and hand position before beginning

Lesson plan— Create a holiday card using Publisher's templates. Make it simple (don't edit text, add only one picture) for students who didn't create these cards in 2nd and 3rd grade. Let those more experienced change as much as they wish. Use this lesson to teach about templates, design, and menus. This project is very easy so shows students how fun and simple computers are.

_____ Open Publisher with icon; select 'Greeting cards'

_____ Scroll to 'holidays' and select a Thanksgiving card (or current holiday)

_____ Select color and font schemes from right sidebar. Try a few before making a choice. Click 'create'.

_____ Encourage those who made cards in 2nd/3rd grade to work with minimal assistance. Change pictures and text or add new pictures and text; edit at least one item on each page. Remember how cards were created in the past. Don't be afraid to experiment.

_____ Those who are new to cards: Don't change text; add one picture

_____ Save (Ctrl+S); save-as to flash drive. Discuss the difference between 'save' and 'save-as'. Print (Ctrl+P)

Option: Have students type a holiday rebus (see next page). This uses skills they know, so have them work independently, with nominal assistance.

Close down to desk top

My computer beat me at checkers, but I sure beat it at kickboxing.
— Emo Philips
The Internet: Where men are men, women are men, and children are FBI agents.
— Anonymous

A THANKSGIVING STORY

Marcy and Mathew were both looking forward to Thanksgiving dinner. They knew they would have baked and a great **BIG** of mashed and sauce and on the cob. They knew they would have a of cranberry sauce and for dessert. BUT, and wanted to have a like all their friends had for Thanksgiving.

So and put on their coats and took their and went out in search of a to have for Thanksgiving dinner. They walked past the and past the and finally came to the . They went inside.

Lesson #12—Holiday Greetings I

Vocabulary	Problem solving	Collaborations
Ctrl *Alt* *Problem solving* *Text box* *Placeholder* *Favorites* *F4*	*What time is it? (hover over clock in systray)* *My program disappeared (is it sleeping on taskbar?)* *My typing disappeared (Ctrl+Z)* *What's 'A' mean at bottom of a text box (text overflowed the text box)*	*Art* *Problem-solving* *Geography*
NETS-S Standards:		
6. Technology Operations and Concepts		

Lesson questions? Go to http://askatechteacher.com

Type to Learn or online typing program—good posture; correct hand position

Remember: Homework due the end of each month

Sign up for word and date for Speak Like a Geek Vocabulary Board (see next pages)

_____ As with problem solving board, students can get definition from family, friends, neighbors or teacher as a last resort. Students are responsible for teaching classmates what word means and using it in a sentence that shows they understand the meaning (i.e., *I like formatting* is not good; *I format my letter by adding borders and pictures* is good)

_____ Review grading (same as prior board—see next pages)

Lesson plan—Create a holiday flier using Publisher's templates. Choose a one-page template and adapt text. Students who did this in 2nd/3rd grade can adjust colors, layout, etc. Use this to teach templates, design, and menus. This project is very easy so I use it to show students how fun and simple computers are.

_____ Explain to students what 'templates' are and have them select one from 'Quick publications'. On right panel, select font and color scheme and push *create*;

_____ Select holiday picture to replace placeholder; edit text (include your name); don't' change font size—Publisher does it automatically

_____ Save to file folder; save-as to flash drive; print

Done? Have websites on class start page that correlate with classroom inquiry into topics. Students who finish the flier can access them.

Close down to desktop (Alt+F4)

There are 10 types of people in the world; those who understand Binary and those who don't.

— Author Unknown

Speak Like a Geek

	Teacher #1	Teacher #2	Teacher #3
Week of Jan 24th			
Week of Jan. 31st			
Week of March 7th			
Week of March 14th			
Week of March 28th			
Week of April 11th			
Week of April 18th			
Week of April 25th			
Week of May 2nd			
	Teacher #1	Teacher #2	Teacher #3

.com			
.gif, .bmp, .jpg			
.gov			
.org			
3-D			
Alignment			
Background/foreground			
Clone			
Color palette			
Crop			
Ctrl+Click			
Data			
Design gallery			
Desk top publishing			
Doc			
Drill down			
Export			
F keys			
Formula			
Handles			
Html			
Hyperlink			
Netiquette			
Network			
Pixels			
Scheme			
Screen shot			
Screen print			
Select-do			
Taskbar			
Toggle			
Tooltip			
Tri-fold			
Washout			
Website address			
WYSIWYG			
Y axis			

Speak Like a Geek Grading

Name: _____

Class: _____

WORD DEFINED: _____

Eye contact _____

Knew word _____

Knew definition _____

Used word in sentence _____

Sentence showed student knew the definition _____

Audience could help if necessary _____

Presence _____

Vocal (no um's, slang, 'something', 'stuff', etc.) _____

Overall _____

Lesson #13-—Holiday Greetings II

Vocabulary	Problem solving	Collaborations
Cyber security *Internet* *Facebook* *Address* *Dot* *'x'*	*Can't exit program (try Alt+F4)* *Screen froze (Is a dialogue box open?)* *My document disappeared (check the taskbar)*	*Spelling* *Grammar* *Critical thinking* *Problem solving* *Presentation skills*
<u>NETS-S Standards:</u> *4. Critical thinking, problem solving*		

Lesson questions? Go to http://askatechteacher.com

Type to Learn or online typing website—good posture; correct hand position
_____ Remember the goal: 25 wpm by the end of the year
Speak like a Geek board—start presentations
_____ Students present their information; take audience questions
_____ Grade based on knowledge, confidence, presence

Lesson plan—Have students type the 'Spell Checker' poem on the next page (pick first or second, depending upon how much time you have). Notice how Word says it's perfect. Go through it and correct spelling, grammar, until it is accurate. Discuss with students the importance of proof-reading, not relying on the computer to catch mistakes.

_____ Open Word. Type poem on next page, making corrections as students type or at the end. There are twelve in the first poem and thirty-three in the second.
_____ When students are done, go over it as a class. Let students discover the mistakes together
_____ Allow this to lead into a discussion on the reliability of spell- and grammar-check.
Internet safety
_____ Discuss internet safety and security with students. What should go on internet? What should they do on the internet? What might they come across that will cause them problems? What is the right way to handle forums, discussion boards, Facebook, etc.?
_____ Give students the rest of the class to visit a variety of internet safety websites (see appendix for examples).
Close down to desktop—Alt+F4

Everything should be made as simple as possible, but not simpler.
— Albert Einstein

The Spell Checker Poem
By Mark Eckman

I have a spelling checquer
It came with my pea see
It highlights for my revue
Mistakes I cannot sea.

I ran this poem thru it
I'm sure your pleased to no
Its letter perfect in it's weigh
My checker told me sew.

An Ode to the Spelling Chequer
by Janet E. Byford

Prays the Lord for the spelling chequer
That came with our pea sea!
Mecca mistake and it puts you rite
Its so easy to ewes, you sea.
I never used to no, was it e before eye?
(Four sometimes its eye before e.)
But now I've discovered the quay to success
It's as simple as won, too, free!
Sew watt if you lose a letter or two,
The whirled won't come two an end!
Can't you sea? It's as plane as the knows on yore face
S. Chequer's my very best friend
I've always had trubble with letters that double
"Is it one or to S's?" I'd wine
But now, as I've tolled you this chequer is grate
And its hi thyme you got won, like mine.

Lesson #14—Publisher Trifolds I

Vocabulary	Problem solving	Collaborations
Trifold	*Can't exit program (Alt+F4)*	*History*
Graphic	*How do I print (Ctrl+P)*	*English*
Text tool	*How do I save (Ctrl+S)*	*Critical thinking*
NETS-S Standards:		
3. Research and information fluency; 6. Technology operations		

Lesson questions? Go to http://askatechteacher.com

Type to Learn or online typing site; Speed quiz next week. No need to practice. If you've been doing homework, with correct posture, entire trimester, you'll be fine.

Speak Like a Geek—continue presentations

Lesson Plan— Students use MS Publisher to create a tri-fold comparing what happened in their life when something else significant was happening around the world. For example, the student was going to Disneyland when Dolly the Sheep was being cloned. Students learn to use templates, add text, pictures, a time line (which can be taught as a separate project) and other design elements. Students are always amazed at what happened around the world.

_____ Students prepared for this project by developing a list of one major event each year of their life and one major event during that same year in history. This can be collected with research, collaboration with friends, or talking with parents.

_____ Open Publisher; select 'Brochures'. Select the first template—it doesn't matter which they pick because we will delete everything.

_____ Delete everything on both sides until all that remains is a blank, scored document. Explain the 3-panel structure of a tri-fold

_____ Enter text box to Panel 1, bottom; type 'This Day in My Life' and student name below it (font size 36, any font, centered)

_____ Copy-paste text box to panel 3 and edit to say, 'This Day in History'

_____ Add color block to top of Panel 1, 3, and entire Panel 2 (see sample next pgs)

_____ Add student picture to top of panel 1 with color block behind to fill white space; add picture of a historic event during student's life to panel 3

_____ Add collage of 3-4 pictures to fill Panel 2 (canted, straight—be creative)

_____ Save to your file folder (Ctrl+S); save-as to flash drive

Save to network folder. Close to desk top (Alt+F4)

"Computers in the future may weigh no more than 1.5 tons." – *Popular Mechanics, 1949 forecasting the march of science*

THIS DAY in MY LIFE

BY Me

THIS DAY in HISTORY

BY Me

PUBLISHER TRIFOLD BROCHURE
Grading Rubric—Fourth Grade

*Your name:*_____

*Your homeroom teacher:*_____

1. Title Page   **4 points**
   a. *Large font*   _____
   b. *Your name and class in smaller font*   _____
   c. *Picture fills white space*   _____
   d. *Border*   _____

2. Collage   **2 points**
   a. *Pictures of world events*   _____
   b. *No white space (color blocks if needed)*_____
   c. *Events are significant and important*   _____
   d. *Spell-check*   _____
   e. *Grammar check*   _____
   f. *Page filled*   _____

3. Page Two   **10 points**
   a. *Border around page*   _____
   b. *Watermark background*   _____
   c. *Timeline*   _____
   d. *Enough bubbles for events*   _____
   e. *Events are significant*   _____
   f. *Spelling*   _____
   g. *Grammar*   _____

4. Overall Professional Look   **4 points**

*How I grade myself:*_____

*Explain:*_____

_____

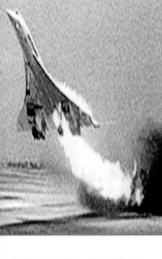

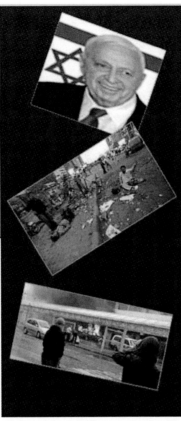

THIS DAY
IN MY
LIFE
By Me

THIS DAY
IN MY
LIFE
By Me

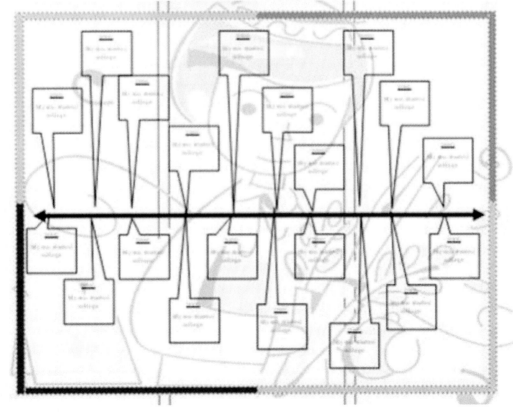

Lesson #15—Publisher Trifolds II

Vocabulary	Problem solving	Collaborations
wpm Grammar-check Trifold Copy-paste Call-out Brochure Handles	My monitor doesn't work (wake up mouse, check power) My computer doesn't work (check power, check plug) My volume doesn't work (check headphones connection)	Spelling Grammar Humanities History

NETS-S Standards:
3. Research and information fluency; 6. Technology operations

Lesson questions? Go to http://askatechteacher.com

Speed quiz—Open Word; add heading—name, date, teacher

_____ Type for 5 minutes, then spell-check for one minute

_____ Type word count at bottom of page

_____ Grade is based on improvement from first quiz (see Lesson 2 for breakdown)

_____ Save (Ctrl+S) and print (Ctrl+P)

Speak Like a Geek—continue presentations

Publisher tri-fold brochure—continue

_____ Add border to Panel 1 and 3, and Page 2. Resize so it fits nicely.

_____ Add a line that bisects Page 2. Use shift key to keep line straight. Make it heavy with arrows at either end. This is the timeline.

_____ Add a call-out to Page 2. Size so it fills about 1/3 of one panel. Copy-paste so there are three call-outs per panel, on all three panels, nine above the timeline and nine below. Pull the tail of each call-out so it touches timeline. The one above and below the timeline should touch each other (see inset).

_____ Fill in each call-out for each year of student's life and history; match tips for same year on timeline

_____ Add student picture as watermark by pasting picture to Page 2, formatting to 'washout' and 'behind text'

_____ Use checklist (see next pages) to check off all required skills

_____ Save (Ctrl+S) to network folder; save-as to flash drive; print (Ctrl+P); fold correctly by matching white sides of pages and folding so cover is out

_____ Done? Go to sponge activities teacher has listed on class internet start page

_____ Close down to desktop

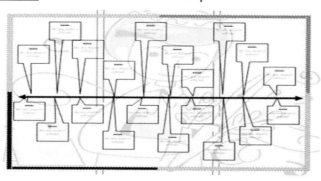

Lesson #16—Graphic Organizers II

Vocabulary	Problem solving	Collaborations
▪ *Design gallery* ▪ *Text box* ▪ *Desk top publishing* ▪ *Drill down*	▪ *My program disappeared (check the taskbar)* ▪ *My document disappeared* ▪ *My typing disappeared (Ctrl+Z)*	▪ *Spelling* ▪ *Grammar* ▪ *Humanities—history*
NETS-S Standards: *2. Communication; 4. Critical thinking*		

Lesson questions? Go to http://askatechteacher.com

Keyboarding—Type to Learn or online typing site; good posture, eyes on screen

Remember: Homework due the end of each month

Speak Like a Geek—continue presentations

Lesson Plan—Use Word's SmartArt to display ideas in a picture format. Students used several in 2nd and 3rd grade. This one uses two: the spokes-and-wheel (from 3rd grade) and the cycle (new). As students work to arrange the pieces, they'll gain a better understanding of the concept and share a picture that appeals to visual learners.

_____ Open Word; add heading at top and title of project, font 14, centered, bold

_____ Insert SmartArt (spokes and wheel); add additional bubbles if needed; add info on Missions (or other topic that collaborates with classroom inquiry) to bubbles. Edit colors to taste; add styles if desired. Students should do this as independently as possible—remember how they did it in 3rd grade

_____ Advanced: Right-click on diagram; select 'format-object' and add picture as background to fit topic (see inset)

_____ Print (Ctrl+P); save (Ctrl+S); save as to flash drive. Ask students what's the difference between 'save' and 'save-as'

_____ Open a new document; this time, insert Cycle SmartArt; add bubbles and text

_____ Add picture to center; wrap and layer. Add text box over picture; edit

_____ Print (Ctrl+P); save (Ctrl+S); save-as to flash drive

Close down to desk top (red X or Alt+F4)

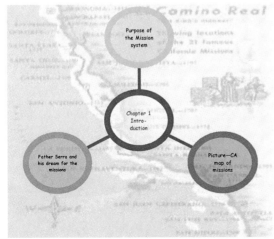
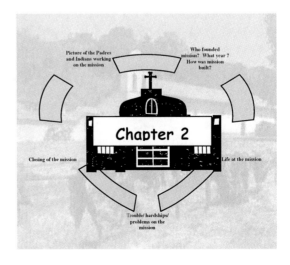

MISSION ORGANIZERS

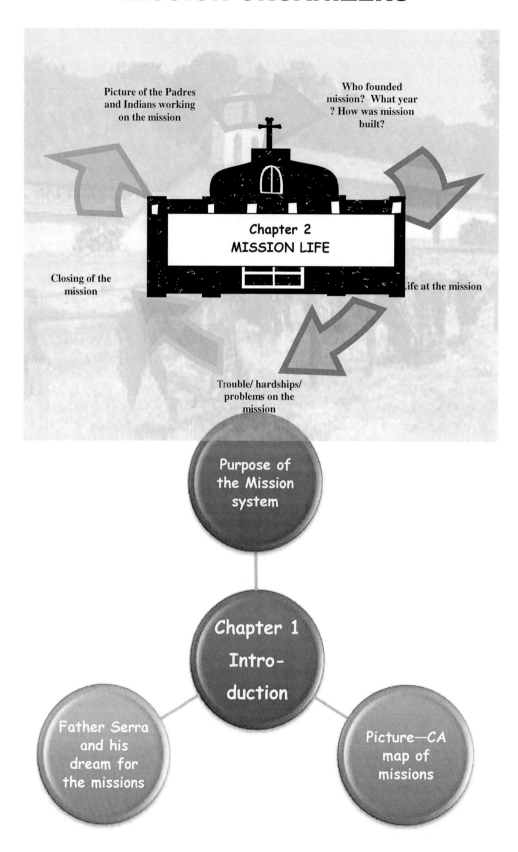

Picture of the Padres and Indians working on the mission

Who founded mission? What year? How was mission built?

Closing of the mission

Chapter 2
MISSION LIFE

Life at the mission

Trouble/ hardships/ problems on the mission

Purpose of the Mission system

Chapter 1 Intro-duction

Father Serra and his dream for the missions

Picture—CA map of missions

Lesson #17—Web 2.0 Vocabulary Study

Vocabulary	Problem solving	Collaborations
Escape Tool bar Column Row Table	My capital won't go off (Is caps lock on?) How to I add a row (tab from last cell of table) What's the date (Shift+Alt+D)	Spelling Grammar Critical thinking Organizing info
NETS-S Standards: 3.c; 6.a		

Lesson questions? Go to http://askatechteacher.com

Type to Learn or online typing website—good posture; correct hand position

Speak Like a Geek—continue presentations

Lesson Plan—create a Tagxedo (or Wordle) using Speak Like a Geek words (or pick words from a class unit of inquiry). Convert boring words into scintillating pictures in five minutes. What a great way for visual learners to remember a topic! See the open letter to teachers about how to use the new Web 2.0 tools to better communicate with parents and teachers (at end of lesson)

_____ Open the internet to Tagxedo (http://www.tagxedo.com)

_____ Enter words from Speak Like a Geek. Have students contribute theirs as others type. The more words on the list, the more filled out the shape will be. It takes about fifty for rubustness, so type a few extras in, too.

_____ Option: Enter words that come to mind when thinking of a book being read in class—about the characters, plot, setting. Include this visual image as part of a book report. See next page for more ideas.

_____ Format with colors, shapes. Save to student file folder. Tagxedos can be embedded into class wikis, teacher's blogs, or any online location to share with students and parents. Once embedded, hovering over a word makes it pop out.

_____ Teach students how to take a screen shot (use Jing or other screen shot utility); save to network folder and Print; save-as to flash drive

Close down to desk top (Alt+F4)

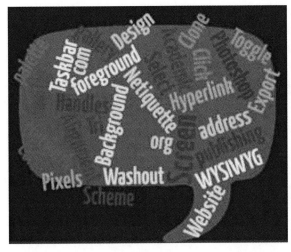

"I have traveled the length and breadth of this country and talked with the best people, and I can assure you that data processing is a fad that won't last out the year."
   - *The editor in charge of business books for Prentice Hall, 1957*

Different Visual Pictures Using the Same Words

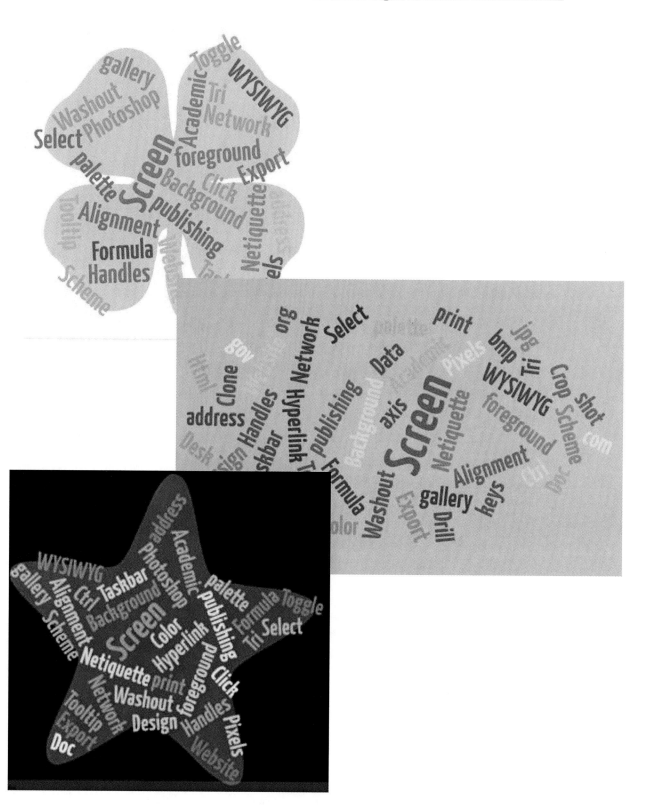

Never Heard of Tagxedo? Read on

If you haven't discovered Tagxedo, you have a treat in store. As its tagline suggests, it is a tag cloud with style. Think Wordle on steroids. Tagxedo takes words and turns them into pictures, with all the options you couldn't find on Wordle. Start with words (or a website, your Delicious links, an RSS feed, a news event or search results for a term). Select colors, fonts, shape. Here's a list of 101 Ways to Use Tagxedo. I've culled my favorites out for you:

- as a discussion of back to school stuff
- what students want to learn about a subject (I'm having my 8th grade Photoshop class create one advising me what they want to learn about photo editing)
- input an essay/book report they've written to see what words pop out as most important. They can then shape it and color it to match the ideas.
- input words from a website they enjoy
- input words from an historic document to see what is the important theme
- any written project normally difficult for visual learners will take on new life with this program
- each student contributes 10 words to describe ****. Write them down on your Smartboard and enter into Tagxedo
- make a Class Tagxedo with the teacher's name larger and students all around him/her
- at the beginning of the school year, ask each student to make a Tagxedo about himself/herself
- make a cover page–turns words about the report topic into a picture
- paste a student essay into Tagxedo. See if other students can work out (a) topic and (b) title of essay. If they fail to do so, this suggests that the essay lacks sufficient focus on the question and student should make some edit, try it again! (thanks *russelltarr)*
- contrast candidates in a Political debate
- summarize a field trip report
- appreciate other languages. Make Tagxedo with non-Latin languages
- teach students about cultures of the world. Add words about a specific culture and shape the Tagxedo like the country. This can also be done for states.
- make a Guess-the-Quote game. Enter all words from a quote and see if the students can figure out the quote.
- brainstorm a topic. Enter all the words about a topic the student comes up with.
- create a synonym word Wall. Look up synonyms of overused words at thesaurus.com. Enter into Tagxedo.
- Track a poll over time. Make a Tagxedo of knowledge on a subject at beginning/middle/end/whatever to show how ideas are evolving.

For more ideas, visit the Daily Tagxedo.

How do you use it?

A Note to My Readers : How I Use Web 2.0 Tools in My Classroom to Communicate with Parents

I've been teaching for over twenty years in different schools, different communities, but one factor transcends grades, classes, and culture: Parents want to be involved with what's going on at their children's school. Parent-teacher communication is vital and in my experience, the number one predictor of success for a student. But parents can't always get in to the classroom as a volunteer and see what's written on the white board. They can't always make the school meetings to hear the comings and goings of the school. Why? It's not lack of interest. More likely, they're working; doing that 8-5 thing that insures the future of their families and pays for their children's college education.

Knowing the importance of parent involvement, I feel that my job as a teacher includes not just the lessons I share with students but keeping my parents informed on classroom happenings. I need to be as transparent as possible, get as much information as I can out to parents in a manner they can understand and a format they can access. If I could tape my classes and post them on YouTube, or offer a live feed during class, I would. But I can't, so I try other creative ideas.

Class website
This is teacher directed, but gives me a chance to communicate class activities, pictures, homework, and extra credit opportunities–all the little details that make up a class–with parents. This is a first stop to understanding what's going on in class.

Class wiki
This is student-directed, student-centered. Students post summaries of their tech class, examples of their work, projects they've completed on the wiki for everyone to share. This way, parents see the class through the eyes of the students. And so do I, which is my way of assuring that what I think happened, did.

Twitter
I love tweets because they're quick, 140 character summaries of activities, announcements, events. They take no time to read and are current.

Emails
I send lots of these out with reminders, updates, FAQs, discussion of issues that are confusing to parents. I often ask if I'm sending too many, but my parents insist they love them.

Open door
I'm available every day after school, without an appointment. Because I have so many other ways to stay in touch, my classroom rarely gets so crowded that I can't deal with everyone on a personal level.

Lesson #18—Cover Pages/Title Pages

Vocabulary	Problem solving	Collaborations
Watermark Title page Cover page Font Double-space Border Save-as	*I can't find my file folder (check log-in. Are you in correct user name?)* *My graph is empty (Did you highlight data?)* *I can't find my document (look in My Documents; maybe you saved it wrong)*	Spelling Grammar History Vocabulary

<u>NETS-S Standards:</u>
3. Research and information fluency; 6. Technology operations

Lesson questions? Go to http://askatechteacher.com

TTL4 or online typing website—remember goal this year: 25 words per minute

_____ Good posture; good hand position

_____ Are you up-to-date on homework?

Speak Like a Geek—continue with presentations

Lesson Plan— Use Quick Publication template to make a fast cover for a report, project, etc., for a classroom unit. With a few adjustments, turn a cover page into a title page (no pictures or watermark). Pay attention to layout, grammar, spelling, design

_____ Open Word; type in title page info (any font, size 36, Bold, centered vertically/horizontally on page, double-spaced); print (Ctrl+P);

_____ For the cover page, add picture (i.e., mission) as watermark; add same picture at bottom of page as decoration; add border—no art borders; print; save to file folder; save-as to flash drive

Close down to desk top (Alt+F4)

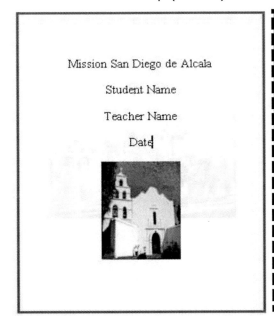

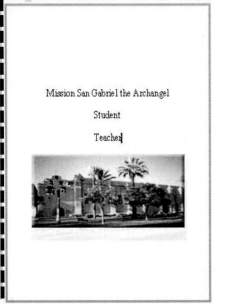

"There is no reason anyone would want a computer in their home."
– Ken Olson, founder of Digital Equipment

Mission San Diego de Alcala

Student Name

Teacher Name

Date

Lesson #19—Storybook in Publisher I

Vocabulary	Problem solving	Collaborations
Toggle *Taskbar* *Flier* *Export* *Jpg* *Digital locker*	*I can't find my file (Are you in correct user name?)* *I can't find my KidPix picture (did you export it or save it?)* *My picture looks weird (Did you resize using side handles?)*	*Spelling* *Grammar* *Composition* *Art* *Problem-solving*
	NETS-S Standards:	
	*1. Creativity and innovation; 2. Communication*	

Lesson questions? Go to http://askatechteacher.com

Type to Learn or online typing site (see appendix for suggestions)
Speak Like a Geek—finish presentations

Lesson plan—Create a ten-sentence story, using characters, setting, plot, rising action, climax and resolution. Have one sentence per page with a picture to communicate the idea. Include a cover and About the Author. Use this lesson to reinforce classroom discussion of story writing and teach students how to use Publisher's design gallery

_____ Each year, students write a tale in technology class that incorporates the elements of a story—plot, characterization, setting, action, climax, and whatever else the classroom teacher highlights. This year, students will use Publisher to create a storybook that uses pictures drawn in KidPix, added with Clipart, or copy-pasted from Google images

_____ Remind students to bring a ten-sentence story (written at home or in class) next week (upload to digital locker if they have these). It should be one sentence per line in a Word doc.

_____ Open Publisher from Start button; select a blank page

_____ Add text box at top for book title—font size 48, any font, any color; add second text box at bottom with student name/teacher in font 18

_____ Save to network; save-as to flash drive. What's the difference? Close Publisher

_____ Open KidPix; draw a picture that fits book's topic. Use at least five colors, only pencil or paint brush—no backgrounds (see sample insets)

_____ Export to network (it will be saved as a jpg picture file); close KidPix

Close Publisher (Alt+F4)

> *All I need now is a computer and a ten year old kid to teach me how to use it.*
> *– Fletch in FLETCH LIVES*

Lesson #20—Storybook in Publisher II

Vocabulary	Problem solving	Collaborations
Export	*I can't exit (Alt+F4)*	*Grammar*
Design Gallery	*I can't print (Ctrl+P)*	*Spelling*
Handles	*How do I add a page to*	*Composition*
Border	*Publisher(insert-page)*	*Problem-solving*
Text box		*Art*

<u>NETS-S Standards:</u>
1. Creativity and innovation; 2. Communication; 4. Problem solving

Lesson questions? Go to http://askatechteacher.com

Type to Learn or online keyboarding website; correct posture; correct hand position

Sign up for Google Earth Board Presentations (see info on next pages); start next week

_____ Students select a date to present and a location from 1) list of places they visited during fourth grade, 2) Wonders of the World, or 3) ???. I've included the list my classes used last year for examples.

_____ Use research skills to find one Fascinating Fact about the location to share with classmates. Allow students to skip a 45-minute homework to give them 45 minutes to do their research.

_____ Fill out all information on study guide (see next pages) including Fascinating Fact.

_____ Grading will be based on criteria listed on rubric (see next pages)

Publisher Storybook—open project. Did students remember their 10-sentence story?

_____ Go to pg. 1; Add KidPix picture (insert-picture); resize with corner handles to fit space available; layer so it is under titles

_____ Advanced: Add design gallery elements to decorate (see sample on above page)

_____ Add twelve pages—10 for sentences, one for 'the end'; one for 'About the Author'

_____ Insert footer with student name and page number (recall how this was done in 3rd grade); remember to close footer when done

_____ Page 2: Insert a border; size to fit around footer. Insert a text box at bottom third of page. Leave top 2/3s for picture. Copy border to pages 3-13. Copy text box to pages 3-11 also.

_____ Page 2-11: Open Word doc with 10-sentence story. Copy one sentence to each page. Adjust font to 18, any font, any color—but keep it the same throughout

_____ Be sure grammar and spelling, capitals, commas, are all correct

Save (Ctrl+S); save-as to flash drive; Close to desktop using with Alt_F4

Once upon a time there was a magical horse named Dreamer

<u>What do you call a computer technician?</u> *It doesn't matter what you call him. He's too busy with the computer to come anyway.*

GOOGLE EARTH BOARD SIGN-UP
Pick a date and a location—so sign your name twice

	Class A	B	C
Week of Dec. 15th			
Week of Jan. 5th			
Week of Jan. 12th			
Week of Jan. 19th			
Week of Jan 26th			
Week of Feb. 2nd			
Week of Feb. 9th			
Week of Feb. 23rd			
Week of Mar. 2nd			

Pick a Location:	Class A	B	C
Egyptian Pyramids			
Great Wall of China			
Stonehenge			
Hagia Sophia, Istanbul			
Leaning Tower of Pisa			
The Eiffel Tower			
Panama Canal			
Taj Mahal			
Victoria Falls			
Ngorongoro Crater			
Mt. Everest			
Ayers Rock			
The Ross Ice Shelf			
Tierra del Fuego			
Straits of Gibraltar			
The Red Sea			
Mt. St. Helens			
San Andreas Fault			
Great African Rift			
Madagascar			
Istanbul			
Siberia			
Death Valley			
Suez Canal			
Vatican City			
The Chunnel			

GOOGLE EARTH BOARD PROJECT

Your name:_____

Your Teacher_____

Estimated time: 45 minutes

1. Write your Google Earth Board location here:_____
2. Write the date of your class presentation here:_____
3. Find your location on Google Earth
4. Print a picture of your location from Google Earth and paste it here:

5. Look up one interesting fact about this location and write it here:

_____

_____

_____

_____

6. When you make your presentation, turn this sheet in to me, filled out
7. Grading will be based on:
    a. Were you prepared on the correct date:
    b. Did you have a picture:
    c. Did you have an interesting fact:
    d. Did you speak loud enough for seat 19 to hear:
    e. Did you avoid 'umms', etc
    f. Did you look the audience in the eye as you talked:
8. You may skip a homework. Put the number of the one you are skipping here:_____

Notes:

- Type the location name in as it is written on the Google Earth Board. That is your best chance of finding it

- Turn off the markers for community notations (the check box that comes up under the 'fly to' locations) before saving the picture

- Save picture as 'file—save—save image' and then select your flash drive

- Turn your 3D buildings on (under 'layers')

- Be sure to pan in so we can clearly see your location or building

- You can get the interesting fact from the encyclopedia, Wikipedia, your parents, or something you learned in class

- If you can't find a location, try the Google Earth Community for a link (for example, use the Community for Ross Ice Shelf)

- If you know the location, you may go there without using the 'fly to' option; just add your own place marker (this might work better for 'San Andreas Fault' and the 'Great African Rift')

GOOGLE EARTH BOARD GRADING

Name: _____

Class: _____

You were prepared with filled-out project sheet _____

Your project sheet had a picture of your location _____

You shared an interested fact with the class _____

You spoke loudly enough for all to hear _____

You seemed knowledgeable _____

You had a calm, confident presence _____

You didn't use vocal cues that showed nervousness_____

You didn't use visual cues that showed nervousness_____

You looked your audience in the eye as you talked _____

Overall impression _____

Lesson #21—Storybook in Publisher III

Vocabulary	Problem solving	Collaborations
Watermark *WordArt* *Desktop Publishing* *Desktop* *Layer* *Google Earth* *Digital lockers* *Save-as, save* *Flash drive*	*My program disappeared (check the taskbar at the bottom; did you save it to network or 'my documents'?)* *The link doesn't work (copy-paste it into the address bar)* *How to I go between Word and Publisher without losing my place (use Alt+Tab)*	*Grammar* *Composition* *Problem solving* *Art*

NETS-S Standards:

1. Creativity and innovation; 2. Communication; 6. Technology operations

Lesson questions? Go to http://askatechteacher.com

Type to Learn or online typing site—correct posture, hand position

_____ Remember monthly homework

Google Earth presentations start today. Demonstrate how and then let students begin

Publisher storybook—open Publisher; open 10-sentence Word story.

_____ Finish adding one sentence to each page (pages 3-11). Use Alt+Tab to toggle between Word and Publisher on taskbar as students copy-paste story. Show students how to use this wonderful shortkey. After each insert, check grammar/spelling.

_____ Page 12: Insert KidPix picture (same one as on front cover); format as washout (or watermark); send picture to back so it layers under WordArt (see inset below)

_____ Add 'The End' in WordArt, layered over watermark

_____ Pages 2-11: Add a picture to each page from clip art, Google images, or drawn in KidPix. Be sure it goes with the sentence of the story, that it says the same as the words do

_____ Resize pictures to fit space on page—about 2/3s of page at the top; stay inside blue print border

_____ Save to file folder; save-as to flash drive as a backup (or digital lockers)

Close program with 'x'; close to desktop

Compaq is considering changing the command "Press Any Key" to "Press Return Key" because of the many calls asking where the "Any" key is.

Lesson #22—Storybook in Publisher IV

Vocabulary	Problem solving	Collaborations
Text box	My project disappeared (use search on under Start button)	Grammar
Print preview		Spelling
Rubric	My project isn't under my network folder (did you save it to 'my documents'?)	Composition
White space		Art
Home row	How do I put a color block behind my pictures? (through 'format' dialogue box)	
Brainstorm		
Pdf	How do I go to 'Print Preview'? (through Print, or file-print)	
Issuu		

NETS-S Standards:
1. Creativity and innovation; 2. Communication

Lesson questions? Go to http://askatechteacher.com

Type to Learn or online typing site—body centered in front of keyboard, elbows at sides

_____ Correct hand position—on home row, curved over keys

Google Earth presentations continue.

Homework—remember to submit monthly

Publisher Storybook—Students will finish today. Open project in Publisher

_____ Students should be done entering story sentences. Check for grammar and spelling errors. Have them continue adding pictures to each page. Think about what the sentence says. What image does that bring to mind? If the first idea doesn't work, try another. Brainstorm with neighbors if needed to come up with an image that conveys the meaning of the sentence.

_____ Size pictures so that no white space shows under or around them

_____ Page 13: Add a text box for 'About the Author'. Tell readers what we should know about you as an author.

_____ Go through rubric checklist (see next pages); print Preview before printing

_____ Ctrl+S to save and then Save-as to flash drive (or back up to digital locker)

_____ Save as a PDF to create a digital book or upload to Issuu (or a similar site) to convert to digital format and share on class wiki or teacher blog

Publisher Storybook
Grading Rubric
Fourth Grade

Creativity

Teacher

Score

1. Title Page
   a. Story title in large font _____
   b. Your name in smaller font _____
   c. KidPix Picture related to topic _____

2. Each Story Page _____
   a. Border _____
   b. Picture appropriate for story _____
   c. One sentence of story _____
   d. Spell-check _____
   e. Page filled (text/pictures) _____

3. The End Page _____
   a. The End in WordArt _____
   b. Watermark of cover _____

4. Overall Professional Look _____

Problem solving: If your screen freezes:
- _"Smash forehead on keyboard to continue..."_
- _"Enter any 11-digit prime number..."_

Publisher Storybook Grading Rubric

Creator:_____

Teacher:_____

Date:_____

1. Title Page _____

  a. *Story title in large font* _____

  b. *Your name in smaller font* _____

  c. *KidPix Picture related to topic* _____

2. Each Story Page _____

  a. *Border* _____

  b. *Picture appropriate for story* _____

  c. *One sentence of story* _____

  d. *Spell-check* _____

  e. *Page filled (text/pictures)* _____

3. About the Author _____

  a. *A few points about yourself* _____

  b. *Border* _____

4. The End Page _____

  a. *The End in WordArt* _____

  b. *Watermark of cover* _____

5. Overall Professional Look _____

Lesson #23—Excel Basics

Vocabulary	Problem solving	Collaborations
▪ *Excel* ▪ *Cells* ▪ *Subpoints* ▪ *Tab* ▪ *Columns* ▪ *Shade* ▪ *Google*	▪ *I can't close (Alt+F4)* ▪ *I can't save to Favorites (click the green plus or check the menu bar at the browser's top for 'Favorites')*	▪ *Science* ▪ *History* ▪ *Composition*
<u>NETS-S Standards:</u> *3. Research and information fluency; 5. Digital citizenship*		

Lesson questions? Go to http://askatechteacher.com

Type to Learn or online typing site—correct hand position

_____ Correct posture—centered in front of computer, legs in front

Google Earth presentations continue.

Lesson plan—review 2ⁿᵈ/3ʳᵈ grade Excel skills (formulas, entering data, changing column/row size, summing/averaging a list of numbers, charting data) and add some easy new ones. Go at the class's pace and show your work on the SmartBoard (or screen). Remind students no one will get everything.

_____ Have students open Excel, add a tab for 'Skills', add student name at top

_____ Display the list of skills on the screen so students can work ahead if they wish, or catch up if they get behind (see inset below). Do as many skills as there's time for in one lesson. Have students practice as you show your work on the screen or SmartBoard (see next page)

_____ Add WordArt title, make a two-line column heading, add the date and time, shade several cells, sort a list of names alphabetically, format numbers as money, add a hyperlink, add a call-out, add an image

_____ Some will get it right away, some will struggle. Whatever they get done is fine.

_____ Save and print when time runs out; close to desktop

KidPix—For those who finish the list

_____ Make a St. Patrick's Day card in KidPix without assistance

_____ Save and print; close down to desktop

Do as many of the following skills as there is time for:
1 Make a two-line heading
2 Insert a WordArt title
3 Widen rows/columns
4 Sort a list alphabetically
5 Autosum a list of numbers
6 Find average of a list of numbers
7 Chart data
8 Format the numbers as money
9 Shade cells
10 Enter a hyperlink
11 Add a call-out to worksheet
12 Enter the date
13 Enter the time
14 Add an image

BASIC EXCEL SKILLS

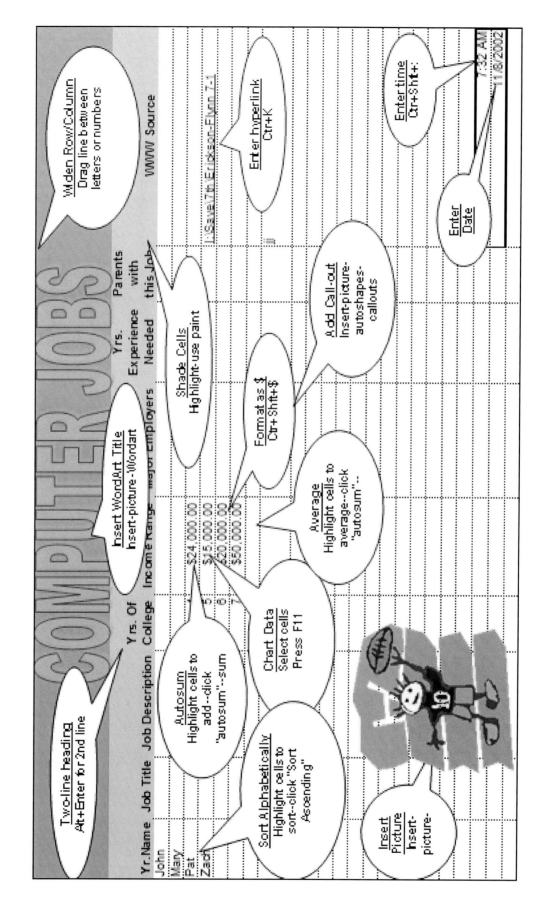

Lesson #24— Internet Research

Vocabulary	Problem solving	Collaborations
Slideshow	How do I add a slide (Insert-slide)	Grammar
Slide	How do I research ("", +, look for qualified websites such as .org, .edu)	Spelling
Background		Sentence construction
Bullets		Science
Storyboard		History
Extensions		Humanities
Credible		Critical thinking

NETS-S Standards:
4. Problem solving; 5. Digital citizenship

Lesson questions? Go to http://askatechteacher.com

Type to Learn or online typing site—correct posture

_____ Correct hand position—on home row, curved over keys, elbows at sides

Google Earth presentations continue

Review problem solving—use examples from Problem Solving Board

Lesson Plan—This project combines a classroom unit with PowerPoint skills. Students research inventors and inventions (or a topic that collaborates with a classroom unit), add information to a storyboard, add that to a slideshow and then format with all the fun pieces that make PowerPoint so exciting to create and watch. Just in time for Open House, too. Include some advanced skills like adding the inventor's picture to the background of his/her slide and adding music to the slideshows—both crowd pleasers. End with presentations to class or parents to practice public speaking skills.

_____ Introduce PowerPoint—purpose, basics, layout; do students remember this from 2nd and 3rd grade?

_____ Show samples of slideshows from last year's fourth graders

_____ Go over storyboard with students. What is a storyboard? Review what's on each slide, what they need to find in their research

Open internet and start researching

_____ Use " " and + to focus research on specific terms

_____ Check extensions for credibility—.org, .gov, .edu

_____ Explain Slides 1 and 2; do Slide 3 as a group—why do people invent? What has been discussed in class on this topic?

_____ Find answers for Slides 4-8. Discuss what is meant by 'why was it needed' and 'difficulties'. What might those be? Use an example so students understand.

_____ Every blank should be filled in (see next pages) by next week

_____ Spend time exploring and reading while browsing

Close down to desktop

POWERPOINT PROJECT—INVENTORS

Your name:_____

Your teacher:_____

Slide 1:   Cover
Slide 2:   Table of Contents
Slide 3:   Why do people invent stuff:
   1._____
   2._____
   3._____
Slide 4:   First of 3 inventors—what they invented:
   1._____(their name)
   2._____(What they invented)
   3._____(Why was it needed)
   4._____(Difficulties inventing it)
Slide 5:   Second of 3 inventors
   1._____(their name)
   2._____(What they invented)
   3._____(Why was it needed)
   4._____(Difficulties inventing it)
Slide 6:   Third of 3 inventors
   1._____(their name)
   2._____What they invented)
   3._____(Why was it needed)
   4._____(Difficulties inventing it)

Slide 7:   Three things invented by accident:

(Howstuffworks.com: science.howstuffworks.com/9-things-invented-or-discovered-by-accident.htm

   1. _____

   2. _____

   3. _____

Slide 8:   What would you invent—steps inventing it:

   1. _____

   2. _____

   3. _____

Slide 9:   About the Author

- *Who do you live with*
- *What are your favorite books*
- *What is your favorite song*
- *What is your favorite activity*
- *What's your dream when you grow up*

Research Sites for Fourth Graders

Quick, safe spots to send your students for research:

1. All-around research site libraryspot.com

2. Dictionary www.dictionary.com

3. Edutainment site—requires subscription
    www.brainpop.com/

4. General info research www.infoplease.com/yearbyyear.html

5. Internet research sites for kids
    http://ivyjoy.com/rayne/kidssearch.html

6. Kids search engine for the internet kids.yahoo.com

7. Math, reading, arcade edutainment www.funbrain.com

8. National Geographic for kids kids.nationalgeographic.com/

9. Nova video programs
    www.pbs.org/wgbh/nova/programs.html

10. Research for kids www.factmonster.com/

11. Research—by grade level
    www.iknowthat.com/com/L3?Area=LabelMaps

12. Research—chapters on subjects http://www.worldalmanacforkids.com/

13. Videos on so many topics www.woopid.com/

14. Research—for kids libraryspot.com/

15. Research—history www.infoplease.com/yearbyyear.html

16. School Tube—learning videos from YouTube. Organized by  topics
    http://sqooltube.com/

17. Science headlines—audio science.nasa.gov/headlines

18. Search the internet www.google.com

19. Thesaurus—a great one www.thesaurus.com

20. World Book Online (subscription required) www.worldbookonline.com/kids

Lesson #25—PowerPoint I

Vocabulary	Problem solving	Collaborations
▪ Wrap ▪ Bullet list ▪ Subtopics ▪ Qualifications ▪ Footer	▪ How do I print? (Ctrl+P) ▪ My shift doesn't work (is your caps lock on?) ▪ How do I make the picture move? (Shift+F5 to play the slideshow)	▪ Grammar ▪ Spelling ▪ Science ▪ Humanities ▪ History
NETS-S Standards:		
2. Communication; 6. Technology operations		

Lesson questions? Go to http://askatechteacher.com

Type to Learn or online typing site—body centered in front of keyboard

_____ Correct hand position—both hands curved over home row

Google Earth Board—continue presentations

PowerPoint presentation on Inventors (or topic which collaborates with class discussion)

_____ Open PowerPoint. Add 9 slides. Have storyboard by student computer

_____ Slide #1—add slideshow title and student name to slide

_____ Slide #2—Title is 'Table of Contents'. Beneath it, in a bullet list, add topics from worksheet. Go over this with students. Add it to a sample that shows on screen or SmartBoard as reference for students. Show them how to decide what goes where on Table of Contents

_____ Slide #3—Add title, Why People Invent Stuff, and list the three reasons you came up with last week

_____ Slide #4-6—Add the title from the storyboard and the information you collected. For the three inventors, the title is the inventor's name.

_____ Slide #7, 9—Follow directions for topics from the worksheet and what you found out in your research

_____ Slide #8: Title is student's invention, with three steps to creating it as bullet list underneath.

_____ Watch grammar and spelling, punctuation and capitals. Keep fonts, sizes, colors consistent throughout slides

_____ Use 'Design' to add backgrounds—left click to add to all and right-click to add to one. Remember what was done last year

_____ Save to file folder; back up to flash drive; close down to desktop

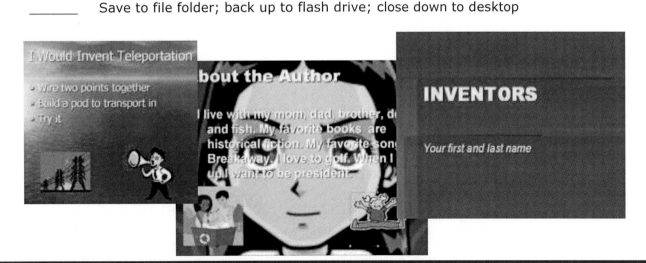

POWERPOINT GRADING RUBRIC

Name_____ Teacher_____

Here's a list of required skills. Check off those you included, and add those you missed. Turn in the grading rubric with your storyboard after your presentation

1. Title slide with author's name   _____

2. Storyboard completed   (turn in with this sheet)   _____

3. Table of Contents includes all slides   _____

4. Each topic covered in slideshow   _____

5. Each slide has heading, animated GIF, clipart   _____

6. Pictures appropriate to text   _____

7. 5 animations, 5 transitions   _____

8. Inventor picture as background on Slide 4-6   _____

9. About the Author with your picture as background   _____

10. Correct spelling   _____

11. Correct grammar   _____

12. All text follows conventions taught in classroom _____

    (word choices, logical thought development, etc)

13. No slang used   _____

14. Slides auto-advance   _____

15. Enough time on each slide for content   _____

16. High level of professionalism   _____

POWERPOINT PRESENTATION GRADING

Name _____

Teacher _____

Date _____

Face audience _____

Talk to audience _____

Introduce yourself _____

Introduce your topic _____

Speak loudly and clearly _____

No 'umms' or stuttering _____

Answer questions _____

Slide show progresses smoothly _____

Understand your topic _____

Lesson #26—PowerPoint II

Vocabulary	Problem solving	Collaborations
▪ *Drop-down menu* ▪ *Slide* ▪ *Animation* ▪ *Scheme* ▪ *Background* ▪ *Image*	▪ *I can't find my project (Start button-search)* ▪ *The computer didn't save my project (Try your back-up on flash drive)* ▪ *What's that red squiggly line? (a misspelled word. Right-click and pick correct spelling)*	▪ *Grammar* ▪ *Spelling* ▪ *History* ▪ *Science* ▪ *Language arts*
NETS-S Standards: *2. Communication; 3. Research and information fluency*		

Lesson questions? Go to http://askatechteacher.com

Type to Learn or online typing site—speed quiz next week

_____ Correct posture—body centered in front of keyboard

_____ Correct hand position—both hands curved over home row position

Google Earth Board—continue presentations

Continue PowerPoint slideshow project

_____ Open PowerPoint; open project saved last week

_____ Continue filling in text; watch spelling and grammar while typing; don't use paragraphs or full sentences—use bullets and phrases

_____ Ctrl+S every ten minutes to save; save early, save often

_____ Use internet search for facts and/or information learned in class to support the topic—don't guess.

_____ Slide #9: Spend time thinking about what an invention is. Discuss with students how inventions come about. They've highlighted several areas of need—once a need is identified, what's the next step? Funding? Get education required to create the invention? Talk to people who are experts on the subject? Have students think this through; assist in these cerebral processes as needed.

_____ Go to Slide #10: Ask students to share where they live, their family, goals, current interests, and what's their favorite book. Beyond that, they can tell us whatever else we should know about them.

_____ Slides 4-6: Add picture of inventor to background (see insert below). Adjust image so it isn't cut off at the top

_____ Slide 9: Add student picture to background (see insert on page above).

_____ Save; save-as to flash drive; close down to desktop

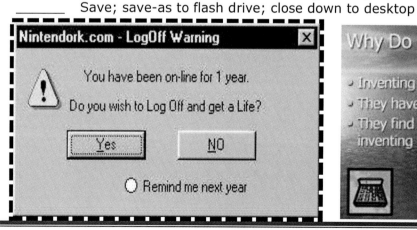

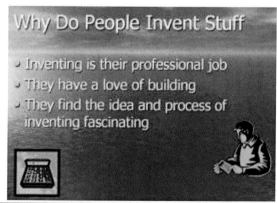

Lesson #27—PowerPoint III

Vocabulary	Problem solving	Collaborations
Multimedia PowerPoint Slide show Transition GIF	My program disappeared (check taskbar) I can't read the webpage I'm in (Ctrl+ zooms in and Ctrl- zooms out)	Grammar Spelling History Science Math
NETS-S Standards: 3. Research and information fluency; 6. Technology concepts		

Lesson questions? Go to http://askatechteacher.com

Type to Learn—warm up for speed quiz

_____ Correct posture—body centered in front of keyboard

_____ Correct hand position—hands curved over home row

Speed quiz—goal is 25 wpm (125 words in 5 minutes)

_____ Open Word; add heading (name, date, teacher)

_____ Type the story (see samples under Lesson 2) for five minutes; don't worry about formatting; don't correct errors—there'll be time for that at the end.

_____ Find word count; type at bottom; take one minute to spell/grammar check

_____ Save (does it matter if student 'saves' or 'save-as'?); print

Continue PowerPoint slideshow project

_____ Open PowerPoint. Open project saved last week

_____ Add Transition to slides by selecting 'transition' from menu bar. Discuss what 'transition' means with students. What's the prefix 'trans-' mean? What are other trans- words? Have students select a transition they like for each slide. Once it's selected, it is on the slide until changed. Push Shift+F5 to watch the slide; push F5 to watch the slideshow from the beginning.

_____ Ctrl+S every ten minutes; save early, save often

_____ To move forward during slideshow, push the spacebar. To have slideshow automatically move forward, go back into Transition screen, select 'auto-advance' on the right and bump time up to eight seconds. Now test the slideshow. It should advance with no hands.

_____ Advanced: Add sounds through 'Transition' ribbon. Make sure they go along with what's happening on the slide. Don't loop them—it's too much noise for the audience when they're trying to listen to you.

Ctrl+S to save and close down to desktop. Why aren't students using 'save-as'?

Titanic Virus: Your computer goes down.

Alzheimer Virus: It makes your computer forget where it put your files.

Child Virus: It constantly does annoying things, but is too cute to get rid of.

Disney Virus: Everything in your computer goes Goofy

Lesson #28—PowerPoint IV

Vocabulary	Problem solving	Collaborations
Slide show 'Greyed out' Drill down Task pane Right-click	My picture got weird (only use corner handles to resize) Slides go too fast (Change speed to slow under Transition)	Grammar Spelling Humanities Math Science

NETS-S Standards:
2. Communication; 3. Research; 4. Critical thinking

Lesson questions? Go to http://askatechteacher.com

Type to Learn or online typing site—correct hand position, body position

_____ Correct posture—legs in front of body, body in front of keyboard

Google Earth Board—continue presentations

Announce winners of 'Keyboard Speedsters' and Fastest Class

_____ 'Keyboard Speedsters' are those students who meet the grade level speed requirement (25wpm) while maintaining correct posture. I award them a prize and post the list on the bulletin board

_____ Fastest Class is the class that has the fastest average speed at their grade level. Discuss what 'average' means and how it is arrived at. Discuss how far this class is behind/ahead and what that means—i.e., each student must improve/slow down .2 wpm. What's *that* mean? Top class gets a prize.

Continue PowerPoint slideshow project

_____ Open PowerPoint; open project saved last week

_____ If students are behind entering text, adding backgrounds, adding transitions, have them catch up when they are ahead of the class or when they have time

_____ Go to Slide #1; go to 'Animation'

_____ See how they're greyed out? To activate, select title of slide. Now, select an animation that is appealing under 'entrance' or 'excite'. Only animate the title—nothing else. Push Shift+F5 to play the slide and see the animation; 'escape' gets out of slideshow

_____ 'Greyed out' is Microsoft's universal way of saying a skill isn't available.

_____ Add animation to each slide. Once added, it's there until changed.

_____ Play slideshow from the beginning. Does it stall? Confirm that all slides show auto-advance for eight seconds. If that's not the problem, go into 'animation'. Select the title that is animated. Change its activation from 'on click' to 'with previous'. Play slideshow again. Does it work now?

_____ Ctrl+S to save. Close down to desktop.

"See Daddy? All the keys are in alphabetical order now."

Lesson #29—PowerPoint V

Vocabulary	Problem solving	Collaborations
Custom animation	How do I capitalize? (use shift key)	Grammar
Page break		Spelling.
Ctrl+enter	My program disappeared? (check task bar)	History
Auto-play		Science
Custom animation	I can't find my project (go to start button-search)	Language arts
Custom path		

NETS-S Standards:
3. Research and information fluency; 5. Digital citizenship

Lesson questions? Go to http://askatechteacher.com

Type to Learn or online typing sites—hands curved over home row, correct posture
Google Earth Board—continue presentations
Continue PowerPoint slideshow project

_____ Students have finished text, backgrounds, animations, transitions

_____ Now add one movie to each slide—sometimes called 'animated GIFs' or 'videos'. Be sure it goes with the topic of the slide

_____ Last: Add a picture to each slide from clip art, Google images or another image file on computer. Again, make sure it goes along with slide's content

_____ Advanced: Add 'Custom Animation' to pictures/words (see inset below). Select one of PowerPoint custom paths or create one. Warn students not to make paths so complicated that they distract from message.

_____ Advanced: Add musical track that plays from beginning to end of slideshow. Be sure to select an MP3. Other formats don't always run as well. Have a group available to pick from.

_____ Done? Practice presentation to be sure it fits within allotted time

_____ Done? Use check list (under Lesson 25) to be sure everything is included. Double check spelling and grammar

_____ Swap slideshows with a classmate who is done and complete a checklist on his/her slideshow

_____ Close down with Ctrl+S.

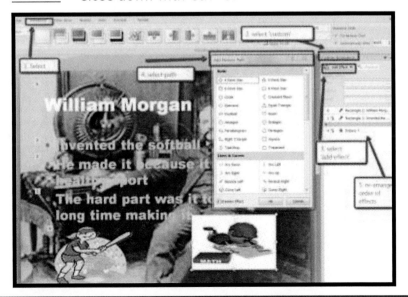

"A computer is like an Old Testament God, with a lot of rules and no mercy."

Vocabulary	Problem solving	Collaborations
• *Auto-advance* • *Transition* • *Animation* • *Mouse click* • *Hard copy* • *Rubric*	• *Computer doesn't work (is power on?)* • *Monitor doesn't work (is power on?)* • *Slideshow is too fast (adjust transition speed and time allowed for each slide)*	• *Spelling* • *Grammar,* • *History* • *Science*
NETS-S Standards: *1. Creativity; 2. Communication*		

Lesson questions? Go to http://askatechteacher.com

Keyboard—Type to Learn or online typing site

_____ Correct posture—body centered in front of keyboard

_____ Correct hand position—hands curved over home row

_____ Go to TypingTest.com (http://www.typingtest.com/) to check typing speed and accuracy. This site counts mistakes and adjusts final wpm to reflect errors.

_____ Select a test; select '3 minutes' and start. Don't stop to make corrections. Type through until time runs out. At the end, test gives a gross and net speed. 'Gross' shows how fast you type if you made no mistakes (see grey number on inset below). 'Net' shows deductions for mistakes (see blue number on inset below). Students love this site, often choosing it over traditional typing sites.

Google Earth Board—continue presentations. Next week is last week.

PowerPoint slideshow presentations—open first slideshow on class monitor or SmartBoard

_____ Explain how grading is done (according to rubric on prior pages). Students keep eyes on audience, glancing at screen only when necessary. Summarize information where necessary and expand where the bullet item is used to remember additional information. Speak loudly so whole room can hear

_____ Audience should pay attention, not fidget, be polite; student grade will be based in part on how good s/he is as an audience

_____ Sound interested and knowledgeable about topic

_____ When presenter finishes, s/he can take up to three questions from audience

_____ Audience must confine questions to what the presenter has discussed

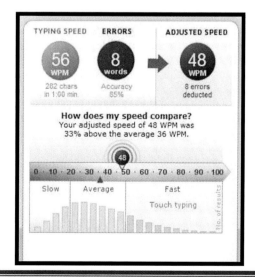

"The box said, WinXP or better required... so I used a Mac!"

Lesson #31—PowerPoint Presentations II

Vocabulary	Problem solving	Collaborations
GIF	Screen froze (is a dialogue box open?)	Grammar
Movie	Can't exit program (Alt+F4)	Spelling
Shift+F5	How do I use a link in a document	Humanities
Esc	(Ctrl+click on blue underlined	History
Auto-advance	words)	
PowerPoint		

NETS-S Standards:
2. Communication and collaboration; 3. Information fluency

Lesson questions? Go to http://askatechteacher.com

Type to Learn or online typing program. Students may want to visit TypingTest.com again. That's fine.

Google Earth Board—finish presentations. Anyone who hasn't yet, will present PowerPoint slideshow presentations

_____ Open student slideshow on classroom monitor or SmartBoard

_____ Review rules with presenter and audience

_____ Students can have parents present for presentations or classroom teacher

_____ Be prepared to move slideshow forward if it gets 'stuck'. Just push spacebar if needed so slideshow seems to progress by itself.

_____ If questions center around why the presenter made a mistake, remind audience that questions are positive, upbeat—that everyone makes mistakes so not to focus on those, rather on what was done right or what sparked the listener's curiosity

_____ Allow three questions from audience. Be sure presenter varies side of the room questions come from, boy/girl, and not the same people who were called on for the last presentation. If time gets short, limit questions to two.

_____ Allow students to sit on the floor in comfortable groups with friends as long as they remain respectful and quiet during presentations

Time at end? Direct students to Inventor/Invention websites listed on class internet start page (see appendix for list of 11; visit AskATechTeacher for updates):

_____ Inventor's Toolbox—http://www.mos.org/sln/Leonardo/inventorsToolbox.html

_____ Inventor's Playhouse—http://inventionatplay.org/playhouse_main.html

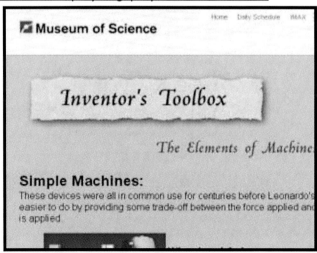

Lesson #32—End-of-Year Challenge

Vocabulary	Problem solving	Collaborations
o *Jeopardy* o *Specialist* o *Generalist*	o *My slideshow stopped (push spacebar)*	o *Spelling* o *Grammar* o *Humanities—history*
NETS-S Standards: 2. Communication; 3. Digital citizenship		

Lesson questions? Go to http://askatechteacher.com

End of Year Challenge—students play a Jeopardy-style game to see who knows the most about different categories of technology (see following pages)

_____ Divide students into teams of four. Students get one week to prepare with the questions. Sometimes, teams assign specialists, some act as generalists. If there is an uneven number of students, assign one as Timekeeper and/or Scorekeeper. These students will always win with the winning team.

_____ Teams go to different 'corners' of the classroom. One member on teach Team is the Speaker—and the only one who can answer questions. S/he will confer with colleagues before answering any question.

_____ The Speaker selects a category (Word Skills, Keyboard Shortcuts, Vocabulary—see study guide on next pages for complete list). Teacher then asks a question from that group. Team has ten seconds to confer and answer. If they are wrong or pass, next team gets a chance. Do not repeat questions. Teams must listen to your question and other Team answers.

_____ Repeat with new Team and new question, but they must select a different category. No category can be repeated.

_____ When time runs out, count points (one point per correct answer), announce winner and award extra credit (or prize). Winning Team gets three additional points for each team member.

_____ Students love this game. If I had time, I'd play it at mid-year also.

_____ Extra: For more excitement, put this into a Jeopardy template (see appendix for sites that can be used for this). Students select from the screen or SmartBoard.

Free time—any websites on class internet start page. Close down with Alt+F4

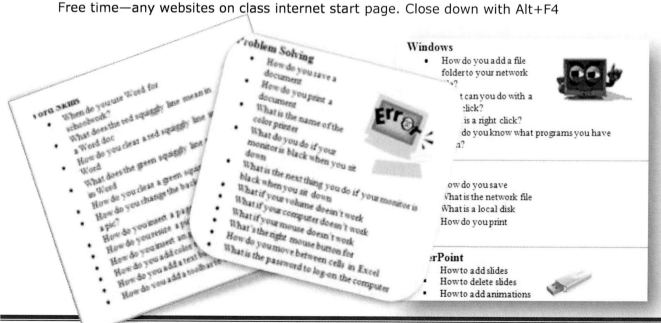

END-OF-YEAR TEAM CHALLENGE

Review the following concepts. These are the questions that will be asked during the Team Challenge—to find the semester's most tech-savvy student!

Word Skills

- When do you use Word for schoolwork?
- What does the red squiggly line mean
- How do you clear a red squiggly line
- What does green squiggly line mean
- How do you clear a green squiggly line
- How do you change image background?
- How do you insert a page border
- How do you resize a picture
- How do you insert an autoshape
- How do you add color to an autoshape
- How do you add a text box

- How do you add a toolbar to your Word
- How do you spell-check a document?
- What is a call-out box?
- How do you add a call-out box to a document?
- How do you make a macro in Word?
- How do you add a watermark?
- How do you add a footer
- How do you double-space
- How do you insert WordArt
- How do you add a border

KEYBOARD SHORTCUTS

- →
- ☺
- Print (Ctrl+P)
- Save (Ctrl+S)
- Copy (Ctrl+C)
- Paste (Ctrl+V)
- Undo (Ctrl+Z)
- Bold (Ctrl+B)
- Italics (Ctrl+I)
- Underline (Ctrl+U)
- Zoom in on a webpage (Ctrl++)

- Zoom out of a webpage (Ctrl+-)
- Exit a program (Alt+F4)
- Insert the current date (Shift+Alt+D)
- Insert the current time (Shift+Alt+T)
- Help (F1)
- New page (Ctrl+Enter)
- Make a graph in Excel (F11)
- Bring back internet toolbar (F11)
- Toggle between taskbar tasks (Alt+tab)

Vocabulary

- Back-up
- Clip art
- Shortcut
- Cursor
- Desktop
- Recycle bin
- Hour glass
- Icon
- Floppy disk
- Folder
- Mouse over
- Task bar
- Drop down menu
- Format
- Font
- Queue
- Handles
- Toolbar
- Scrollbar

- Wizard
- Multimedia
- Explorer
- PC
- Netiquette
- Footer
- Thesaurus
- Page Break
- Hyperlink
- Active window
- I-beam
- Initialize
- Dialogue box
- Kilobyte
- Pixel
- Search engine
- Browser
- Thumbnail
- Tile

- Drill down
- Right-click menu
- Log-on
- Protocol
- Alt
- F4
- Cc
- Win 7
- Caps lock
- Monitor
- Footer
- Animation
- Transition
- GIF
- JPG
- .com
- .edu
- .net
- .org

- Auto-play
- Auto-advance
- Place saver
- Bullets
- Numbered list
- Crop
- Print preview
- Washout
- Watermark
- Import
- Export
- Data
- Textbook
- Worksheet
- Default
- Internet address
- Network
- Back button
- Forward button

- Printkey
- Wrap
- Search bar
- Address bar
- Google (verb)
- Hits
- Synonym
- Flash drive
- USB port
- Jump drive
- Thumb drive
- Digital locker
- Upload

Lab Rules

- Name three lab rules
- How often should you save?
- How do you print from the internet?
- What does "Respect everyone's work" mean?
- When can you eat in the lab?
- What internet site can you go on?
- What is proper posture at the computer?
- When can you plagiarize?

- When do you not have to give credit for information from the internet?
- Who is to blame if you miss work or homework or forget your book?
- Which four letter words are specifically prohibited ('can't', 'won't')
- If you don't know a lab rule, does that mean you aren't responsible for following it?
- When is it OK to go into someone else's file folder?
- What if you miss a class?
- When can you touch someone else's equipment?

Problem Solving

- How do you save a document
- How do you print a document
- What is the name of the color printer
- What do you do if your monitor is black when you sit down
- What is the next thing you do if your monitor is black when you sit down
- What if your volume doesn't work
- What if your computer doesn't work
- What if your mouse doesn't work
- What's the right mouse button for
- How do you move between cells in Excel

- What is the password to log-on the computer
- What is the user name to log-on the computer
- How do you find the date on the computer
- What is the keyboard shortcut to auto-insert the current date
- How do you search for a file
- What if your capitals are stuck on
- How do you fix a weird looking resized image
- What if F11 doesn't create the chart in Excel
- What's the keyboard shortcut to close a program
- If a double-click doesn't work, what do you do
- What if you accidentally delete words/pictures
- What do you do if your desktop icons are messed up
- What if your Start button disappears
- Name two things you do if your screen seems frozen

Internet

- How do you copy-paste from the internet
- How do you send an email from your home
- How do you request a Return Receipt for email
- What is a search engine
- What is the 'Back' button
- What is the 'Forward' button
- What is the 'Home' button
- What is the 'Refresh' button
- What's the difference between the search bar and the address bar
- What is the Address Bar

- What's the 'History' tool
- How to bookmark a site
- How to print (copy-paste to Word first)
- How do you add to Favorites
- What is Favorites
- When can you go on the internet at school
- Name one address we have visited on the internet
- How do you attach a document to an email
- How do you select the best site from a search engine

Publisher

- How do you insert a page
- How do you add text

- What is 'Design Gallery'
- What is the 'Task Pane'?

- How do you add a border
- How do you insert a picture
- How do you insert picture from KidPix
- How do you move material from one page to another
- Why use Publisher?

- Name four projects we did in Publisher
- How do you add a Table of Contents
- How do you add a footer
- How do you add the page number to the footer
- How do you enlarge a page

Graphics

- How do you crop a picture
- How do you change a picture background
- What is Photoshop
- How do you wrap text around a picture
- How do you resize a picture
- How do you move an image around page

- How do you insert from a file
- How do you insert from the internet
- How do you insert from clipart
- When you insert a clipart image, where does it go (the blinking cursor)

Windows

- How do you add a file folder to your network file?
- What can you do with a right-click?
- What is a right click?
- How do you know what programs you have open?
- How do you change the wallpaper?

- What if the taskbar is gone?
  - What if the start button is gone?
  - What are Function keys?
  - Name something on a right click menu
  - How do you toggle between tasks on taskbar

Basics

- How do you save
- What is the network file
- What is a local disk
- How do you print

- Name 5 parts of the computer
- How do you 'Print screen'

PowerPoint

- How to add slides
- How to delete slides
- How to add animations
- How to add transitions
- How to add moving pictures
- How to add GIF's
- How to add sounds
- How to change background

- How to use pictures for backgrounds
- How to insert pictures from clipart
- How to insert pictures from the internet
- How to insert pictures from your home file folder
- How to insert hyperlinks
- How to auto-advance slides

Excel

- How to enter data
- How to graph data
- How to alphabetize names
- How to auto-sum
- How to average numbers
- How to add numbers
- How to subtract numbers
- How to multiply numbers
- How to divide numbers

- How to widen columns
- How to widen rows
- How to format text
- How to insert a picture
- How to add the date
- How to add the time
- How to change the worksheet name
- How to change the tab color
- How to add a worksheet

HOMEWORK #4-1—via email

Not submitted: *0 pts*
Submitted: *5 pts*
Subject line protocol: *-1 pt*
Late: *-1 pt.*

Send me an email from home with:
- o Your name
- o Your email address
- o Your parents' names
- o What you want to learn about computers
- o What you know about computers

HOMEWORK #4-2—hard copy

Not submitted: *0 pts*
Submitted: *5 pts*
Subject line protocol: *-1 pt*
Late: *-1 pt.*

Go onto the technology class page. Take a screen print of 'What We Did This Week'. It can be any week available, just so I recognize it as a screen print (with the tool bars and task bar showing). Copy-paste it into the body of an email and send.

HOMEWORK #4-3—via email

Not submitted: 0 pts
Submitted: 5 pts
Subject line protocol: -1 pt
Late: -1 pt.

Hints below are from last year's Fourth Graders to help you thrive this year.
Read them; type five of your favorites into an email and send them to me.
Stop after 45 minutes

Hints for Incoming Fourth Graders

Hard things/Things I don't like

- Memorizing vocabulary words
- Excel, graphs
- PowerPoint, Publisher
- Problem-solving
- Missing things when I didn't pay attention
- Type to Learn
- Typing faster
- Home row keys
- Homework drills
- Making tables
- Slideshow presentation
- Changing font size
- Not understanding something
- Spell-check and grammar-check
- Timeline
- Difficult to catch up when you get behind
- Accidentally deleting something

Easy things/My Favorite things

- KidPix
- Word, writing stories
- Type to Learn
- PowerPoint, Publisher
- Internet to help with homework
- Learning to type faster
- Computers do what I tell them
- Learning new things about computer
- Keyboard shortcuts
- Searching the internet
- Googling pictures
- Playing around with the programs
- Making cards
- Doing fun stuff
- Using them when you need them
- FREE's

Advice

- Listen or you will be left behind
- Do your homework—it helps a lot!
- Do your homework a day early
- Fourth grade is harder than third
- Computers can be fun
- Do your best work
- Ask questions
- Practice Practice Practice!
- Never give up
- Take care of the computers
- Don't raise your hand when the teacher is talking
- Don't miss class

HOMEWORK #4-4—*hard copy*

Not submitted:	*0 pts*
Submitted:	*5 pts*
Subject line protocol:	*-1 pt*
Late:	*-1 pt.*

Draw a map of the computer lab with KidPix, Paint, or even a blank sheet of paper (see example below). Add the two doors at either side so you can orient the rest of your drawing and then add items 1-7. Don't spend more than 45 minutes. When you're done, turn in the hard copy to my in box or email the digital copy.

1. *Put a red 'X' where you sit in class*
2. *Put a blue 'X' on traits of a good learner (My Attitudes, My Profile)*
3. *Put a pink 'X' where homework is posted.*
4. *Put a green 'X' by Lab Rules*
5. *Put a yellow 'X' by the printer and printer basket*
6. *Put a black 'X' by Earth Map*
7. *Put an orange 'X' where you can see the skills you will learn this year.*

HOMEWORK #4-5—via email

Place this printout next to your keyboard. Type the lines, keeping your eyes on the text. Practice hitting the RETURN key without looking. DON'T CORRECT MISTAKES! You are trying to learn the keys NOT how to fix mistakes. This will increase your speed and your accuracy. Stop after 45 minutes. **If you are practicing at home regularly you should be seeing a big difference in your typing speed and accuracy.** Paste into body of email and send to me.

1. a;sldkfj a;sldkfj a;sldkfj a;sldkfj a;sldkfj
2. aa ;; ss ll dd kk ff jj a;sldkfj fjdksla;
3. asdf jkl; asdf jkl; fdsa ;lkj fdsa ;lkj
4. aa ;; ss ll dd kk ff jj aa ff jj dd kk ss ll aa ;;

5. aj sk dl f; aj sk dl f; ;f ld ks ja fj dk sl a;
6. la ls ld lf ka ks kd kf ja js jd jf ;a ;s ;d ;f
7. aj ak al a; sj sk sl s; dj dk dl d; fj fk fl f;
8. asd fjk ;lk fds sdf kl; lkj dsa sdf kl; fds lkj

9. as as ask ask asks asks ad ad ads ads as ask ads
10. sad sad dad dad fad fad lad lad all fall dads fads
11. all lad ask fad lass ad dad all fall ads
12. salad salsa alfalfa salad salsa alfalfa

13. as a lad; ask a dad; all fall; a sad lad;
14. a fall; a flas; all fall; all dads; ask dad;
15. a fall ad; a sad lass; as a dad; sad dad;
16. aa ;; ss ll dd kk ff jj a;sldkfj a;sldkfj

HOMEWORK #4-6—via email

Not submitted: *0 pts*
Submitted: *5 pts*
Subject line protocol: *-1 pt*
Late: *-1 pt.*

Place this printout next to your keyboard. Type the lines, keeping your eyes on the text. Practice hitting the RETURN key without looking. DON'T CORRECT MISTAKES! You are trying to learn the keys NOT how to fix mistakes. This will increase your speed and your accuracy. Stop after 45 minutes. **If you are practicing at home regularly you should be seeing a big difference in your typing speed and accuracy.** Paste into body of email and send to me.

```
kit sit fit fist kid it lit hid hill fill sill
jag hag lag leg glad gas gag sag egg  leg keg
nat nan den fan land hand sand fan tan than hen

tin sing kind king hint shine gain tag link
the then these this that thin than think
night sight light fight height night light
gang fang hang sang gang fang hang sang

a tall tale; a keen knight; a fine sight
he felt he needed the things at the sale
the lads asked the king at the east gate
he is a fine dad; she said he needs his kind
he had a kite; sing a little; he has a fish;

fail sail jail laid hail tail nail fail
sealing dealing keeling kneeling healing
if it is in the its a in at is it the then
is the; in the; if the; let the; see the;
fin din sin gin kin sit lit kit hit fit
```

HOMEWORK #4-7—via email

Not submitted: 0 pts
Submitted: 5 pts
Subject line protocol: -1 pt
Late: -1 pt.

Place this printout next to your keyboard. Type the lines, keeping your eyes on the text. Practice hitting the RETURN key without looking. DON'T CORRECT MISTAKES! You are trying to learn the keys NOT how to fix mistakes. This will increase your speed and your accuracy. Stop after 45 minutes. **If you are practicing at home regularly you should be seeing a big difference in your typing speed and accuracy.** Paste into body of email and send to me.

lol lol lol lol lol lol lol lol lol lol lol lol
lot log load hold done too to go do so of on old
gone tooth jolts fool good song sold fold told gold

frf frf frf frf frf frf frf frf frf frf frf frf frf
red rag ran far her rat tar the free jar dart dirt fir
first rake hard rail free are hare hair her red dear

aLa aLa aLa aLa aJa aJa aKa aKa aLa aLa
aHa aHa aIa aIa aOa aOa aNa aNa aNa aHa
He His Ned Nan Jan Nate Jake Is Lee Ned I Ira

note nose none done fore sore tore soar dare lone
tone gone roan thorn goat one rote fir far tar jar
for her; for those; for this; for their; for him; for the

He asked Jan to send the letter to Kari;
Here are the things that she sent to Nan;

is it to the go for he she that is the or and this these
He is; Hal sat; Nan gets; Is it; Jake is; Go to the;

HOMEWORK #4-8—via email

Not submitted: 0 pts
Submitted: 5 pts
Subject line protocol: -1 pt
Late: -1 pt.

Place this printout next to your keyboard. Type the lines, keeping your eyes on the text. Practice hitting the RETURN key without looking. DON'T CORRECT MISTAKES! You are trying to learn the keys NOT how to fix mistakes. This will increase your speed and your accuracy. Stop after 45 minutes. **If you are practicing at home regularly you should be seeing a big difference in your typing speed and accuracy.** Paste into body of email and send to me.

mom mud mam jam more time mow mad met mat
bib bit bid rib bad book bob rob sob bow
cod cup cut cow can cat tack call cot cell

most meet team same mail man comb con car
cab cob crib clam much cost cast computer
beat beam bell ball bowl bad brim better

be bet cram crab cab mince crime can munch
Right now is the time to finish the job.
One of the men will be able to sing now.
Bob brought the cat and the dog to school.
She did not like to eat hamburgers with cheese.
He did bring his lunch to the game.
Where is the crab soup that he cooked.
Oscar would like his teacher to grade his test.

HOMEWORK #4-9—via email

Not submitted: 0 pts
Submitted: 5 pts
Subject line protocol: -1 pt
Late: -1 pt.

Websites you can use:

http://www.multied.com/Thistory.html
http://www.infoplease.com/yearbyyear.html

Year	World Event	My Event
2011	Osama bin Laden died	My son joined the Army
2010	The Winter Olympics took place	We got a new dog
2009	Johanna Sigurdardottir takes office as Iceland's first female prime minister.	
2008	Bobby Fischer died	My daughter graduated from USNA
2007	Barry Bonds surpassed Hank Aaron as the all-time home run hitter in American baseball history	My dog got cancer
2006	President Mahmoud Ahmadinejad announces that Iran has successfully enriched uranium	
2005	France and the Netherlands reject the EU constitution	My son started college!
2004	500 killed in Morocco quake	My daughter started college!
2003	7 astronauts die in space shuttle Columbia disaster	I started a new hobby—writing
2002	Taliban overthrown in Afghanistan	I started teaching at SMAA
2001	Terrorists attack the USA	
2000	The human genome is deciphered	

HOMEWORK #4-10—via email

Not submitted: *0 pts*
Submitted: *5 pts*
Subject line protocol: *-1 pt*
Late: *-1 pt.*

Place this printout next to your keyboard. Type the lines, keeping your eyes on the text. Practice hitting the RETURN key without looking. DON'T CORRECT MISTAKES! You are trying to learn the keys NOT how to fix mistakes. This will increase your speed and your accuracy. Stop after 45 minutes. **If you are practicing at home regularly you should be seeing a big difference in your typing speed and accuracy.** Paste into body of email and send to me.

fvf fvf fvf fvf fvf fvf fvf fvf fvf
five cave give gave value ever van
aza aza aza aza aza aza aza aza aza
zap zany lazy zero zip zone zoom zest

zig zag zip zinc zone dozen graze faze
have have hive heave hover above brave
gave give have hive zoo size maze gaze
doze quiz froze frizz dive leave vase

a small car may not have as much zip.
a hive of bees came after the lazy dove.
it was a very hard quiz so he failed.
he gave me a zebra and waved goodbye.
she was very lazy and never saw the zoo.

HOMEWORK #4-11—via email

Not submitted: *0 pts*
Submitted: *5 pts*
Subject line protocol: *-1 pt*
Late: *-1 pt.*

Place this printout next to your keyboard. Type the lines, keeping your eyes on the text. DON'T CORRECT MISTAKES! You are trying to learn the keys NOT how to fix mistakes. This will increase your speed and your accuracy. Stop after 45 minutes. **If you are practicing at home regularly you should see a big difference in your typing speed and accuracy.** Paste into body of email and send to me.

```
juj juj juj juj juj juj juj juj juj juj juj juj juj
sws sws sws sws sws sws sws sws sws
jug run dug hug rug jut just our use sun fun
sew saw sow wet were wig win was won we

few sat was wag were fte drag wade dare date
junk use us fuss our four down town work two
had his use two who whose new now when was
week while with won will wall would want well
few sat was wag wig were wade rude waste wet

we are; we will; we want; we think that;
the of to and in for we that is this our
of the; in the; to the; for the; on the;
it is; with the; of our; and the; it is;
all an are at do for has he his if in it

we should; we would; we think; we shall;
Jane John Joe Jennifer June Jan Jewell Jill Josh

Let her go.  I will too.  Ned wants one also. I had a ft. of wire
I sang.  Josh jogged.  Helen did the work. Nan went to Ohio U.
J. L. was in the jet. Kathy went to the store.
```

HOMEWORK #4-12—via email

Not submitted:	*0 pts*
Submitted:	*5 pts*
Subject line protocol:	*-1 pt*
Late:	*-1 pt.*

Write a reflection on computer projects, homework, and the class in general. Write one paragraph per topic (projects, homework, and class). Each paragraph must have 3-5 sentences.

Make sure you use good grammar and spelling. Spend about 45 minutes on this project.

HOMEWORK #4-13—via email

Place this printout next to your keyboard. Type the lines, keeping your eyes on the text. Practice hitting the RETURN key without looking. DON'T CORRECT MISTAKES! You are trying to learn the keys NOT how to fix mistakes. This will increase your speed and your accuracy. Repeat the lines, until you've typed for 45 minutes. **If you are practicing at home regularly you should be seeing a big difference in your typing speed and accuracy.** Paste into body of email and send to me.

sip sap lap lip slop plop flop flip slip
life, like, hike, sit, hit, pit, sip,
That is, He will, I do, She did, It eats,
To Ron, Ed, Sal, Fred, Don, Dan, Sal, Dean,
part past please repair tape trip trap
president past pest spare parts hip ship
She is sending the letter to Leon.
He did not go to the store.
Where are the notes for the test.
Let us know when the order gets here.

HOMEWORK #4-14—via email

Not submitted: 0 pts
Submitted: 5 pts
Subject line protocol: -1 pt
Late: -1 pt.

Type and review the Word concepts and email to me. If it's a question, type the answer. If there are any you don't know, find the answer, ask a friend, or come ask me!

Word Skills

- What does the red squiggly line mean in a Word doc
- When do you use Word for schoolwork?
- How do you clear a red squiggly line in Word
- What does the green squiggly line mean in Word
- How do you clear a green squiggly line

- How do you insert a page border
- How do you resize a picture
- How do you insert an autoshape
- How do you add a text box
- How do you spell-check a document?
- How do you add a watermark?
- What are the home row keys

KEYBOARD SHORTCUTS

- →
- ☺
- Ctrl+P = Print
- to exit a program (Alt+F4)

- to insert the current date (Shift+Alt+D)
- to insert the current time (Shift+Alt+T)
- Help (F1)
- Undo (Ctrl+Z)

HOMEWORK #4-15—via email

Not submitted: *0 pts*
Submitted: *5 pts*
Subject line protocol: -1 pt
Late: *-1 pt.*

Place this printout next to your keyboard. Type the lines, keeping your eyes on the text. Practice hitting the RETURN key without looking. DON'T CORRECT MISTAKES! You are trying to learn the keys NOT how to fix mistakes. This will increase your speed and your accuracy. Stop after 45 minutes. **If you are practicing at home regularly you should be seeing a big difference in your typing speed and accuracy.** Paste into body of email and send to me.

1. see lee fee dee led fed dead feed sea seas
2. had has he she dash lash hall heed hal
3. tea set let jet fat sat tell tall talk eat
4. feel keel leaf jell seal seek leased fed

5. hash heal shell sheds sashes ashes heals
6. jets least let fat east feat teak sat eat
7. task these dash steel leads teeth feet eat
8. lakes the these fee seals jest seek feats

9. seek the deal; at least ask a dad; a fast jet;
10. dad had the jet; he has a deal; the sale;
11. the last jet; see the last lad; the fast seal;
12. the teeth; these lads; a deal; these salads;

HOMEWORK #4-16—via email

Not submitted: *0 pts*
Submitted: *5 pts*
Subject line protocol: *-1 pt*
Late: *-1 pt.*

Place this printout next to your keyboard. Type the words, keeping your eyes on the text. Practice hitting the RETURN key without looking. DON'T CORRECT MISTAKES! You are trying to learn the keys NOT how to fix mistakes. This will increase your speed and your accuracy. Stop after 45 minutes. **If you don't know how to type in columns, just type one long column. That's still full credit.** Paste into body of email and send to me.

Sad	Cat	Wax	Fun	Hat	Men	Fee	Hum
Bad	Fat	Tax	Run	Mat	Pen	See	Mum
Bar	Rat	Sea	Nun	Pat	Ten	Bet	Yum
Car	Bug	Tea	Cup	Bay	Let	Get	
Far	Rug	Bed	Pup	Day	Net	Set	Dad
Tar	Rag	Fed	But	Hayden	Pet	Vet	Had
Sat	Wag	Red	Camp	Hen	Yet	Wet	Mad
Vat	Sat	Wed	Lamp	Lid	Bid	Hop	Pad
Raw	Vat	Bee	Fear	Rid	Did	Mop	Nag
Saw	Raw	Jam	Hear	Pie	Dig	Pop	Ham
Bat	Saw Map	Can	Near	Pie	Jig	Tot	Bug
Pan	Nap	Fan	Year	Big	Pig	Cow	Dug
Ran	Rap	Man	Sear	Cot	Wig	How	Rug
Tan	Tap	Zip	Pear	Dot	Dip	Now	Hug
Van	Zap	Lip	Wear	Hot	Rip	Wow	Jug
Cap	Fog	Kip	Jeer	Lot	Sip	Box	Bun
Lap	Hog	Fix	Fall	Not	Tip	Fox	Fun
Moo	Log	Mix	Hall	Pot	Fire	Jock	Nun
Zoo	Bog	Six	Tall	Rot	Hire	Dock	Run
Coo		Dog Oil	Wall	Put	Wire	Jump	Sun

HOMEWORK #4-17—via email

Not submitted:	*0 pts*
Submitted:	*5 pts*
Subject line protocol:	*-1 pt*
Late:	*-1 pt.*

Place this printout next to your keyboard. Type the lines, keeping your eyes on the text. Practice hitting the RETURN key without looking. DON'T CORRECT MISTAKES! You are trying to learn the keys NOT how to fix mistakes. This will increase your speed and your accuracy. Stop after 45 minutes. **If you are practicing at home regularly you should be seeing a big difference in your typing speed and accuracy.** Paste into body of email and send to me.

```
fvf fvf fvf fvf fvf fvf fvf fvf fvf
five cave give gave value ever van
aza aza aza aza aza aza aza aza aza
zap zany lazy zero zip zone zoom zest

zig zag zip zinc zone dozen graze faze
have have hive heave hover above brave
gave give have hive zoo size maze gaze
doze quiz froze frizz dive leave vase

a small car may not have as much zip.
a hive of bees came after the lazy dove.
it was a very hard quiz so he failed.
he gave me a zebra and waved goodbye.
she was very lazy and never saw the zoo.

he she it to the if or and up we can do
the where why when this that then they
if he is to do this job for us, he must.
I can use the large raft if i ask first.
They are sure that i can type fast.
```

HOMEWORK #4-18—via email

Read the following story. You'll probably feel like it was written for younger children than 4th grade—and you're right! The reason is:

- You don't know anything about the characters
- You don't know anything about the setting
- The words are too simple.

Fix this story and email it to me. Describe Coyote and Tree within the story. See the bubble I inserted as an example. Describe the setting—see my bubble for an example. Use the thesaurus to select more advanced words than those that are underlined.

> *Coyote was very old. His fur was mangy and falling out in spots. And his bright white teeth had yellowed with the diet of grasses he ate. He had...*

"Mr. **Coyote** was getting very <u>old</u> and had to be more careful for his own safety. He had been <u>walking</u> for hours and hours through a <u>beautiful</u> **valley** when he came upon a large **tree**. Mr. Coyote was very tired and wanted to <u>rest</u> but he also needed to be safe. He kindly asked the tree, "Please open up so I can rest safely in your care".

> *Its trunk was craggy and thick, and its arms spread wide over the grass as though welcoming Mr. Coyote.*

HOMEWORK #4-19—hard copy

Not submitted: 0 pts
Submitted: 5 pts
Subject line protocol: -1 pt
Late: -1 pt.

Complete the Word Search below. When you're done, scan it into your computer and email it or turn in the hard copy. Either way is full credit.

```
G D K C I L C E L B U O D H J O S L M P M K
L R T O B I D T X N B L I N K I N G H V L E
L A E D V Z M U L L D P E I D D F R J H U X
N B X T E Y B Z Y R R D L Q H L S M A W K A
H U G I T S O A N J E R O S R U C D S O A Y
W N I X N E K S A T I T L U M D D P M G D P
S E Y Z W M U U B K D P K P K R Z I N L T O
E M I Y O B N Q M H J N C A E D P O V D S C
L G I Z D L E Y I O P Y P S J M C Y O P P Y
D I N X L H M Q C T G B S Y S I B U O A Q S
N F B Y L P N D S K E B E O U U B Y T W G E
A Q K G I O W Y J A A N X B P L P D Z T K T
H P A O R P O R H R E D J Q E R U W E O A R
Q U E V D M D V E K H N Z U O G F A T O L U
C T R E F Q N M M W W O S T S O A T G L I O
V K B J Z Q P S V R Q P O S R C V E O B G C
A C E R F O O G A T A C S M D Q O R E A N V
F A G E F N R P T C O U A D P A R M L R M P
R B A T A O D U E L I T B S M H I A G I E O
V C P O Z O N K M S Z X E V H I T R G O N R
Y E Q O O W Y T Q S B Y J G T V E K O N T C
T B T F S E A R C H B A R I V N S V T Q P S
```

address bar	drop-down menu	multitask	toolbar	double click
alignment	favorites	netiquette	watermark	drill down
back-up	font	page break	wrap	search bar
blinking	footer	PC	icon	toggle
courtesy copy	format	protocol	jpg	cursor
crop	GIF	handles	menu bar	double-space

HOMEWORK #4-20—via email

Outline notes from one of your classes and email it to me. Use bullets or numbered list. Reference the book, the subject, the page, so I can find them. Add pictures to make it more interesting.

HOMEWORK #4-21—via email

Type a letter to me telling me what I should tell next year's fourth graders about technology class and email it to me. Include:
- What you like about computers
- What you find difficult
- What your favorite computer activity is
- What your least favorite computer activity is
- What advice you would give incoming fourth graders to help them thrive in computer class

HOMEWORK #4-22—via email

Not submitted: *0 pts*
Submitted: *5 pts*
Subject line protocol: *-1 pt*
Late: *-1 pt.*

Have your parents type a letter to me telling me what I should tell next year's fourth grade parents about technology class and email it to me. Include:

- Tips and secrets
- Things that they found out too late
- Things that should be explained earlier and aren't
- Things that are especially valuable
- What advice they would give incoming fourth grade parents

The ISTE
National Educational Technology Standards and Performance Indicators for Students

1. **Creativity and Innovation**
   Students demonstrate creative thinking, construct knowledge, and develop innovative products and processes using technology. Students:
   a. apply existing knowledge to generate new ideas, products, or processes.
   b. create original works as a means of personal or group expression.
   c. use models and simulations to explore complex systems and issues.
   d. identify trends and forecast possibilities.

2. **Communication and Collaboration**
   Students use digital media and environments to communicate and work collaboratively, including at a distance, to support individual learning and contribute to the learning of others. Students:
   a. interact, collaborate, and publish with peers, experts, or others employing a variety of digital environments and media.
   b. communicate information and ideas effectively to multiple audiences using a variety of media and formats.
   c. develop cultural understanding and global awareness by engaging with learners of other cultures.
   d. contribute to project teams to produce original works or solve problems.

3. **Research and Information Fluency**
   Students apply digital tools to gather, evaluate, and use information. Students:
   a. plan strategies to guide inquiry.
   b. locate, organize, analyze, evaluate, synthesize, and ethically use information from a variety of sources and media.
   c. evaluate and select information sources and digital tools based on the appropriateness to specific tasks.
   d. process data and report results.

4. **Critical Thinking, Problem Solving, and Decision Making**
   Students use critical thinking skills to plan and conduct research, manage projects, solve problems, and make informed decisions using appropriate digital tools and resources. Students:
   a. identify and define authentic problems and significant questions for investigation.
   b. plan and manage activities to develop a solution or complete a project.
   c. collect and analyze data to identify solutions and/or make informed decisions.
   d. use multiple processes and diverse perspectives to explore alternative solutions.

5. **Digital Citizenship**
   Students understand human, cultural, and societal issues related to technology and practice legal and ethical behavior. Students:
   a. advocate and practice safe, legal, and responsible use of information and technology.
   b. exhibit a positive attitude toward using technology that supports collaboration, learning, and productivity.
   c. demonstrate personal responsibility for lifelong learning.
   d. exhibit leadership for digital citizenship.

6. **Technology Operations and Concepts**
   Students demonstrate a sound understanding of technology concepts, systems, and operations:
   a. understand and use technology systems.
   b. select and use applications effectively and productively.
   c. troubleshoot systems and applications.
   d. transfer current knowledge to learning of new technologies.

Internet Websites

a. Chess
b. Computer lab favorites
c. Edheads—Activate your mind
d. Edutainment games and stories
e. Edutainment
f. First Thanksgiving
g. Geography game—geospy
h. Geography—geonet game
i. Google Earth—free download site
j. History—videos of events
k. How stuff works
l. Inventors and inventions Misc. Links
m. Math/LA Videos by grade level
n. National Gallery of Art—for kids
o. National Geographic
p. Nova video programs
q. Research—a great dictionary
r. Research—a great thesaurus
s. Research—facts
t. Research—for kids
u. Research—for kids
v. Research—history
w. Science headlines—audio
x. Search the internet
y. Spelling—-games to learn class words
z. Stories for all ages
aa. Stories for all ages
bb. The White House—for kids
41. Typing program—a graduated course

Specific to Units

Animals

1. Animals
2. Animal games
3. Classify animals
4. Google Earth—animal habitats
5. Google Earth—endangered animals
6. Google Earth—African Animals

Art

1. Art—Make a monster
2. Drawminos
3. Clay animations
4. Metropolitan Museum of Art
5. Minneapolis Institute of Arts
6. Mr. Picassa Head
7. Museum of Modern Art
8. National Gallery of Art—for kids

Biomes

1. Biomes of the World
2. Breathing earth—the environment
3. Build a Prairie
4. Extreme Organisms on Earth
5. Observe Different Climate Zones
6. World's Biomes
7. Virtual tours

CA History

1. CA Historical Society
2. CA History Overview
3. CA History Review
4. CA Indian Basketry
5. Ca Native Americans
6. CA Tribe Map

7. Golden Gate Bridge
8. Historical Fiction List
9. History Home on the Internet

CA Missions

1. CA History-Missions
2. CA Mission Life
3. CA Mission Pictures
4. CA Mission Pictures—all Missions
5. CA Missions Foundation
6. CA Missions
7. CA Missions
8. CA Missions
9. CA Missions
10. CA Missions Online
11. CA Missions Studies
12. Daily Life at Missions
13. Father Serra
14. Father Serra—more
15. Father Serra—still more
16. Mission Site Collection
17. Mission Timeline
18. Santa Barbara Mission
19. The Spanish Missions
20. Tour CA Missions with Google Earth

CA Regions

1. CA Landscape
2. CA Regions
3. CA's Regions
4. Images of CA Regions
5. PowerPoint of CA Regions

Cultures

1. First Thanksgiving
2. World National Anthems

Geography

Geography Games III

Globe (lat and long)

1. Big Bang to present
2. Continental drift
3. Explore the Colorado River
4. Find your Longitude
5. Geography Games
6. Geography Games II
7. Geography Pop-ups
8. GeoSpy Game
9. Glen Canyon Dam
10. Latitude-Longitude Map Game
11. Latitude-Longitude Quiz
12. Learn the states
13. Los Angeles River Tour
14. Map activity
15. Map Labeling Activity
16. Place the state on a map
17. Rivers
18. Rivers Seen from Space
19. USA Puzzle
20. World Geography
21. Zambezi River

Gold Rush

1. Gold Rush History
2. Gold Rush
3. Gold Rush 2
4. Gold Rush: 49ers

5. Gold Rush: Fun
6. Gold Rush: Untold Stories
7. Gold Rush—PBS movie
8. San Francisco Virtual Museum

History

1. Colonial America
2. Egyptian Madlibs
3. Egyptian Pyramids
4. George Washington
5. Greeks-Romans
6. History Central
7. History for Kids—facts, games, quotes
8. Mt. Vernon
9. Native American Conflicts
10. Oregon Trail—virtual tour
11. Pharaoh's Tomb Game
12. RR—inventing
13. RR—modern marvel
14. RR transforms America
15. White House

Holidays

1. Earth Day
2. Groundhog Day

The Human Body

1. Human Body Games
2. Inside the Human Body
3. Virtual weather, machines and surgery

Inventions

1. A Guide to Inventions
2. Famous Inventors
3. Famous Inventors—by Kids
4. Famous Inventors—List of
5. Great Inventions
6. Inventing a New Pencil
7. Invention at Play
8. Inventions: Transportation
9. Inventor's Toolbox
10. Inventors and Inventions
11. Inventors Hall of Fame

Keyboarding Practice

1. Finger jig practice game
2. Free typing tutor
3. Keyboard challenge—adapted to grade level
4. Keyboard practice—quick start
5. Keyboard test—quick, adjustable
6. Keyboard—free online typing course
7. Keyboarding Fingerjig—6 minute test
8. Keyboarding for Kids
9. Keyboarding practice
10. Keyboarding resources listed
11. Keyboarding—alphabet rain game
12. Keyboarding—barracuda game
13. Keyboarding—bubbles game
14. Keyboarding—Dance Mat Typing
15. Keyboarding—full online course
16. Keyboarding—games
17. Keyboarding—lessons
18. Keyboarding—lessons and speed quiz
19. Keyboarding—more lessons
20. Keyboarding—must sign up, but free
21. Keyboarding—quick start
22. Keyboarding—speed quiz
23. Keyboard—practice with a game
24. Krazy keyboarding for kids
25. Online practice
26. Online practice—quick start
27. Online typing course
28. Online typing lessons
29. Online typing lessons — even more
30. Online typing lessons — more
31. Typing program—a graduated course

Language Arts

1. Analyzing, reading and writing literature
2. BiteSize—Reading, Writing, Grammar
3. Create a Wordle
4. Grammaropolis
5. Thinking Skills—Riddles

Math

1. A Plus Math
2. Arithmattack
3. Interactive Math Lessons for Grades 2-6
4. Learn Multiplication facts—the fun way
5. Math Basics
6. Math Basics Plus
7. Math Concepts—and more
8. Math—Grids
9. Math Grids II
10. Math Playground
11. Math Practice Test
12. Math—by Grade Level—lots of stuff
13. Math—Wild on Math—simple to use
14. Mental Math Drills
15. Minute Math
16. NumberNut Math Games
17. Quick Math
18. Quick Math II
19. Speed Math
20. Test Your Math
21. Virtual Manipulatives and Tessellations

Matter and Energy

1. Bill Nye, the Science Guy
2. Changing States of Matter
3. Cool Science
4. Matter Changing States
5. Matter
6. Simple machines
7. Solids and Liquids
8. States of Matter Game

Miscellaneous

1. All About America
2. Minyanland
3. Transcontinental Railroad video
4. Modern Freight Trains
5. Inventions: Transportation
6. School Tube—videos Organized by topics
7. 360° views from around the world

Poetry

1. Analyzing, reading and writing literature
2. Cinquain Poems
3. Favorite Poem Project
4. Fourth Grade Poems
5. Funny Poetry
6. Glossary of Poetry Terms
7. Poetry Engine
8. Poetry forms
9. Poetry with a Porpoise
10. Shel Silverstein
11. Shaped Poems—fun
12. Magnetic Haiku poetry
13. Robo Poem
14. Musical poem—you write poem, add music

Research

1. Dictionary.com
2. Edutainment site—requires subscription
3. General info research
4. Great Research sites
5. History Central
6. Internet research sites for kids
7. Kids search engine for the internet
8. libraryspot.com

9. Math, reading, arcade edutainment
10. National Geographic for kids
11. Nova video programs
12. Research for kids
13. World Almanac for Kids
14. School Tube—learning videos
15. Science headlines—audio
16. Thesaurus.com
17. Virtual Library
18. World Book Online

Rocks and minerals

1. Cyber Prospecting
2. How Rocks are Formed
3. Rock Cycles
4. Rock Scavenger Hunt
5. Rocks for Kids
6. Rocks

Sacramento
CA State Capital Museum

Science

1. Electric Circuits Game
2. Fantastic Contraption
3. Forests
4. Geology
5. Great Science site
6. Molecularium
7. Moon—We Choose the Moon
8. Moon around
9. NASA For Kids
10. NASA Kids Club
11. Ology Sites
12. Plant games
13. Plant life cycle
14. Satellite Fly-bys—by zip code
15. Science activities for the mind
16. Science games
17. Science Games II
18. Science Games—Bitesize
19. Science Stuff
20. Solar System in 3D
21. Stardate Online
22. Virtual Field Trips
23. Virtual tour (with pictures) of a zoo
24. Virtual tours
25. Virtual tour—undersea
26. Virtual weather, machines and surgery
27. Wonderville

Spanish

1. Spanish resources
2. Spanish Stories

Technology

1. Computer basics
2. Computer Basics II
3. Computer parts
4. Computer puzzle
5. Faux Paws Internet Safety
6. Find the Technology
7. Internet Safety
8. Netsmartz
9. Organize technology (drag and drop)
10. Parts of the computer
11. Videos on Computer Basics K-6
12. Who are your online friends?

USA

1. All About America
2. USA Games
3. USA Puzzle
4. US History Map Game

Word Study

1. Dolch Site Word Activities
2. Grammar games
3. Grammaropolis
4. High-frequency words—hangman
5. High-frequency words—practice
6. Spelling practice—use with spelling words
7. Stories with Dolch Words
8. Visuwords
9. Vocabulary Fun
10. Word Central—from Merriam Webster
11. Word Videos

A Christian site

The Animated Bible

For Teachers

1. Animations, assessments, charts, more
2. 10 Tech Alternatives to Book Reports
3. Children's University
4. Create a magazine cover
5. Create free activities, diagrams in Flash!
6. Creative Tools
7. Crossword Puzzle Maker
8. Easy Techie Stuff for the Classroom
9. Easy-to-navigate collection
10. Environmental footprint
11. Glogster—posters
12. Google Earth Lesson Plans I
13. Google Earth Lesson Plans II
14. Google Earth in Math Curriculum
15. Hollywood Sq/Jeopardy Templates
16. How to Videos for Web 2.0
17. K-8 school-related videos. Tons of them
18. Make digital posters
19. Mapping ideas with tag clouds
20. Online quizzes you create, online grades
21. Password creator
22. Posters—8x10 at a time—simple
23. Print Large Posters in 8x10 bits
24. Print Posters One Page at a Time
25. Publish the magazines
26. Pupil Tube
27. Puzzle maker—for study guides, etc.
28. Online tools (Web 2.0)—all free
29. Teach vocab, prefixes/suffixes, more
30. Shelfari—share books with students
31. Slideshows created on line
32. Slideshare—upload PowerPoint; share
33. Slideboom—upload PowerPoints; share
34. Slideshow upload with Authorstream
35. Tools for studying writing
36. Training videos
37. Lots of poetry sites
38. Turn pictures into Videos—Easily
39. Turn short stories into books

Index

More Technology Books
for your Classroom

Name
Address
Email
Phone Number

Which book?	Price (print/ebook/Combo)	How Many?	P&H ($2.99/4.50 /bk)	Total
Kindergarten Tech Textbook	$18.99/$14.99/$30.99			
1st Grade Tech Textbook	$22.99/$14.99/$32.99			
2nd Grade Tech Textbook	$22.99/$14.99/$32.99			
3rd Grade Tech Textbook	$22.99/$14.99/$32.99			
4th Grade Tech Textbook	$22.99/$16.99/$34.99			
5th Grade Tech Textbook	$22.99/$17.99/$36.99			
6th Grade Tech Textbook	$25.99/18.99/$38.99			
K-6 Combo (all 7 textbooks)	$143.97/$99.97/$219.99			
55 Tech Projects—Volume I	$32.99/$16.99/$47.99			
55 Tech Projects—Volume II	$32.99/$16.99/$47.99			
Toolkit Combo—VI and II	$59.99/$36.99/$85.97			
16 Holiday Projects				
19 Posters for the Tech Lab	$6.99 (digital only)			
38 Web 2.0 Articles	$2.99 (digital only)			
	Total			

Fill out this form (prices subject to change).
Email Zeke.rowe@structuredlearning.net.
Pay via Paypal, Amazon, Google Ebooks or
pre-approved school district PO.
Questions? Contact Zeke Rowe.

Structured Learning
http://structuredlearning.net
AskaTechTeacher.com
Zeke Rowe